STORIES FROM CEP's FIRST TEN YEARS

WALKING THE UNION WALK

JAMIE SWIFT

STORIES FROM CEP's FIRST TEN YEARS

WALKING THE UNION WALK

JAMIE SWIFT

Communications, Energy and Paperworkers
Union of Canada

Between the Lines
Toronto, Canada

Walking the Union Walk

© 2003 Communications, Energy and Paperworkers Union of Canada

First published in Canada in 2003 by

Between the Lines	and	Communications, Energy and Paperworkers
720 Bathurst Street, Suite 404		Union of Canada
Toronto, Ontario M5S 2R4		301 Laurier Avenue W.
www.btlbooks.com		Ottawa, ON K1P 6M6
		www.cep.ca

National Library of Canada Cataloguing in Publication

Swift, Jamie, 1951 –
        Walking the union walk : stories from CEP's first ten years / Jamie Swift.

ISBN 1-896357-74-1

1. Communications, Energy and Paperworkers Union of Canada – History. 2. Trade-unions – Canada – History. I. Communications, Energy and Paperworkers Union of Canada. II. Title.

HD6528.T32C64 2003b	331.88'11384'0971	C2003-905237-0

Co-ordinated by Robert Hatfield

Edited by Robert Clarke

Designed and produced by Working Design

Scans by Starfish Communications

Printed and bound in Canada by Transcontinental Printing and Graphics

Between the Lines gratefully acknowledges assistance for its publishing activities from the Government of Canada through the Book Publishing Industry Development Program.

Foreword

BY BRIAN PAYNE

THE PHOTO ON THE COVER of this book is displayed with pride in many CEP offices. It shows the 1993 Ottawa demonstration against the North American Free Trade Agreement (NAFTA) and the other job-killing policies of the discredited Mulroney government. This amazing event took place less than a year after our founding convention. The demonstration helped to define what CEP would be all about: a union that is proactive inside and outside the workplace; a union that isn't just talking the talk, but is walking the walk.

In our first decade we have defined ourselves as a militant trade union. Anyone who checks the record will know that. Anyone who reads the stories in this book will realize that. "Did we win all our fights?" Well, we may not have won them all, but there is not an employer in any industry in this country that doesn't know that we will stand up and fight if they throw down the gauntlet.

We defined ourselves appropriately at the outset. We put together not just a large union, but a union that would make a collective commitment that goes beyond a particular industry. CEP is a large union active in many industries. We are a multifaceted organization from coast to coast to coast. We have created solidarity across the union.

But we are also the media union in this country. We are the paper union. We are the energy union. We are the telecommunications union. We don't forsake our commitment to individual groups. We provide specialized, expert support to our members in every sector.

Sometimes the support needed is strike support. Over the first ten years we paid out almost $100 million from the Defense Fund, not counting special assessments and local donations. We are proud that all members involved in strikes and lockouts have always received their Defense Fund entitlements.

Our Defense Fund allows us to stand up and be counted in the face of every employer in the country: from Abitibi to CBC to SaskTel. Our membership strength gave us the ability to stand on the picket line for nine and a half months in Western Canada during the Fletcher Challenge strike. It gave us the ability to fight Bell Canada. You will read these stories in this book.

Beyond the workplace, the ambulance tour was one of our first national campaigns. We are continuing this work with our current medicare campaign. We have an ongoing campaign to reduce working hours, and we continue to

▲ CEP NATIONAL PRESIDENT BRIAN PAYNE:
"We put together not just a large union, but a union that would make a collective commitment that goes beyond a particular industry.... We support people, even if they are not our members, when it's the right thing to do."

take on specific issues such as softwood lumber and the privatization of public utilities such as electricity.

We aim to do what's right. We support people, even if they are not our members, when it's the right thing to do. For example, Joanne Stubbins's daughter Robyn Lafleur died as a result of injuries she sustained in an explosion at Esquire Canada. CEP supported this mother's campaign to turn a tragic death into something positive by working to prevent similar deaths from happening in the future. You'll find other examples in this book.

We take our role in the international labour movement seriously too. We have industries that are being swallowed up by global corporations. As a result, we are putting together international trade union networks to deal with particular multinational corporations. We participate in trade union secretariats that regroup members in our jurisdictions around the world. Our Humanity Fund provides a way that CEP members can work with other trade unionists on international issues. You'll read about the work of the fund in this book.

We are also involved in the push-back against unfair global trade arrangements that are being foisted on workers around the world. Some one thousand CEP members participated in the spring 2001 demonstrations at the Summit of the Americas in Quebec City. We were key players in the protests against the 2002 G8 meeting in Kananaskis, Alta. Our board and convention have endorsed this kind of activism. We are proud that we are doing it. The activism represents an important way of working to protect our livelihoods, and it is an important role that we play as citizens.

Our merger in November 1992 combined cultures. We had more than one view on issues. It gave us an opportunity to take those histories and those experiences, put them in the blender, shake them up, and come out with a good mix.

I see CEP's first ten years as a huge celebration, a tremendous coming together, an overpowering feeling of solidarity. We're pretty proud of our first ten years – but just watch us in the next ten!

Acknowledgements

THIS BOOK COULD NEVER have been undertaken, let alone completed, without the help of the countless CEP members, officers, and staff who took the time to offer me their stories and insights. It is also very much the result of a co-operative effort. CEP's Véronique Derny-Gauvreau, Lisette Desjardins, Joseph Gargiso, Diane Goulet, James Kinkaid, Marie-Andrée L'Heureux, Pierre Rose, Fred Wilson, and President Brian Payne made major contributions. Don Bouzek produced the video that accompanies the book, exchanged ideas, and kindly drove me here and there in search of more stories. Antonia Banyard and Kris Klaasen of Working Design made the book look handsome; Robert Clarke, my eternal editor, made it read well.

Finally, I'd like to thank Bob Hatfield of the CEP's national office. His sound advice, unflappability – and above all his good humour – kept the project on the rails. It's his book as much as it is anyone's.

Jamie Swift
Kingston, July 2003

Introduction:
THE HABIT OF SOLIDARITY

IT WAS 6:30 ON A MARCH MORNING when we went for coffee at Hector's place on the hill overlooking the mill. As we sat down Hector asked Sandy if he wanted breakfast.

"No thanks. I'm working nights."

"Got another job?"

"Why don't you *&#!@*&?"

Hector laughed. So did Sandy. Every morning an informal coffee club convened at Hector's place. It was a spot where people in Dalhousie, N.B., could chew over the news of the day and kid each other about just about anything, including how little the papermakers worked compared to everyone else down the hill at the mill. Sandy Beckingham, the president of Local 263, laughed about how it has always irritated the managers to see the papermakers sitting around, casually opening their lunch boxes to ponder what their next snack should be.

"But it gets them even more pissed off when we're working," explained Sandy, a shrewd observer of the power relations at the mill. Nothing gets the bosses more anxious than a prolonged paper break.

Sandy's lunch box is covered with union stickers. The biggest one, right on top, says "Remember Westray."

◀ *Sandy Beckingham has coffee at Hector's store, up the hill from the mill in Dalhousie. The long-time union activist describes himself as "a citizen of the planet."*

D. BOUZEK

It's not a matter of training sessions or bringing in consultants with Power Point presentations. "You learn by sharing knowledge," says Sandy Beckingham.

"When we're relaxing it means that the machines are working and they know they're making money. When we're hard at it, that means there's no paper being made."

When there is a paper break, the papermakers jump around like monkeys, exchanging a complex set of hand signals because it's too loud to talk. There are hundreds of valves amidst the kilometres of pipe in a paper machine. Even after twenty-five years Sandy is still learning the job. It's not a matter of training sessions or bringing in consultants with Power Point presentations. "You learn by sharing knowledge."

Hector has watched the goings-on at the mill for as long as Sandy has worked there, preferring his small *dépanneur*/restaurant to shift work. He could have caught on at the mill back in the 1970s when they were actually hiring. As with many CEP workplaces, the average age is in the late forties. Hector said he noticed that when the union negotiated shorter hours and longer shifts, the papermakers began carrying bigger lunch boxes. Sandy's lunch box is covered with union stickers. The biggest one, right on top, says "Remember Westray."

Building a union: coast to coast

I SPENT THREE MONTHS on the road in the spring of 2002, visiting the places where CEP members live and work, collecting stories from the new union's first ten years.

I had had some contact with the union since the beginning, and before that with the Canadian Paperworkers Union. After completing a book on forestry in Canada, in the mid-1980s I was invited to speak at a meeting where the union was considering the issue of spraying the forest with pesticides to kill insects. An industry apologist was the other speaker, and he thought it was a good idea. I didn't, but I didn't know how the mill workers would react to the not-so-subtle message about bugs threatening jobs. A fellow from the floor who looked like a cross between a hippie and a biker took the microphone and soon had people bending over with laughter and shaking their heads. Sandy Beckingham, who describes himself as a part-time papermaker and union activist and a "citizen of the planet the rest of the time," set the tone of the discussion. He made fun of the logic of zapping the entire forest ecosystem in an attempt to kill off insects that were proliferating as a result of industry's government-approved logging practices.

When I met Sandy again in Dalhousie, his stories were just as funny, his insights just as interesting. He described the importance of his participation on the board of New Brunswick's Workers Investment Fund and how he had heard that employers just across the bridge in Quebec had even approached unions asking to get organized so that they could have access to the multi-billion-dollar Quebec Federation of Labour's Solidarity Fund. I also asked him what – aside from spending time in meetings and dealing with the complaints of the membership – was involved in being a local union activist. He summed it up with a single word: Trust.

He said the key to being a union leader was to be "honest and up front" with people. "If someone asks you a question and you don't know the answer, say so."

When I began this project I wondered just how well the new union had jelled. I was already aware that the CEP was the product of the merger of three medium-sized unions: the Communications and Electrical Workers of Canada, the Energy and Chemical Workers Union, and the Canadian Paperworkers Union. None of them were growing in their traditional sectors, having reached a plateau where their costs were rising and their membership was stable or declining. The only way to get out of that box was to build a bigger one. As soon as the new box was created it got even bigger when several large media unions joined up.

It is no easy task to combine different organizational cultures and traditions into a single whole, especially when the organizations involved are under attack from anti-labour governments and ever more aggressive and powerful corporations. Add to that the difficulty of forming a national union that must work out the complex relations between Quebec and the rest of the country. Few other institutions – aside from the federal government and the Catholic Church – even bother trying.

My travels took me from St. John's, Nfld., to Powell River, B.C. I visited the regional headquarters where dozens of people worked and went to local union offices that were little more than cubicles tucked into the corners of factories. Some workplaces where thousands of people had once earned a living now employed only a few hundred. Often the members were middle-aged men, a reflection of the traditional industrial settings that CEP's founding unions had organized. Many of them were in small hinterland communities like Dalhousie, though an increasing number were in big-city offices and plants, the sites of more recent organizing successes.

One of the people I met along the way was Max Michaud, who hails from what he describes as the Republic of Madawaska, also in Northern New Brunswick. CEP's Atlantic region vice-president is proud that this part of the country is CEP territory. The union has twenty-two CEP worksites in Edmunston, where he started out as a steam-plant operator in 1966.

MURRAY MOSHER

▲ *Max Michaud, Atlantic vice-president. The Michaud Recipe has three elements: service, education and organizing.*

It is no easy task to combine different organizational cultures and traditions into a single whole, especially when the organizations involved are under attack from anti-labour governments and ever more aggressive and powerful corporations.

Bell has clear-cut the ▲
jobs of the telephone
operators while
stonewalling the pay
equity claims of the
women who built the
phone company.

"The only people we don't have are the police, the nurses, and the lawyers," he said, laughing. "As soon as a new industry comes in, we get a call right away because everyone is CEP and they all know us."

Max has an instinctive grasp of what it takes to build a successful union, even in a region where unemployment is always high. When I talked to him in May, he also proved to have an unerring memory for numbers.

"In the Atlantic, 3.4 per cent of our members have taken a course in the last sixteen months. We gave weekend courses in at least twenty-five different locations. And in the past six months we increased our membership in the region by 14 per cent."

The Michaud Recipe is elegantly simple. It has three ingredients: service, education, and organizing. The union is there to provide service to its members, and the best way to do that is not to have staff reps driving all over but to have well-educated shop stewards and local union officers who can take care of most things by themselves. This frees up staff time to concentrate on organizing new members who can in turn start to take courses so they can look after their own day-to-day needs.

"Staff can't be always stuck at a grievance at the third step because the officers of the local and the shop stewards don't know how to do the job. You have to educate people to do that. Staff can work on campaigns and organizing – any union that doesn't organize is not going to survive."

That reminded me of something I noticed when visiting places where CEP represents paperworkers, energy workers, and telephone workers. I would ask about the average age of the membership. The answer was usually "late forties." I would ask how many years' service the average member had. The answer was usually, "Oh, twenty-three or so." When I would ask if the workforce had grown in recent years, I was greeted with a laugh by some; others looked at me as though I was from another planet.

The CEP is like many other unions. It has an aging membership base in sectors that are not expanding. In many cases, employers are eliminating the jobs.

In Masson, Quebec, Richard Lahaie told me that, at thirty-nine, he is one of the younger workers in the mill where most of the men have put in at least twenty-five years. The thermo-mechanical pulping (TMP) area looks like a giant stainless steel kitchen. The operators sit at computer consoles in a control room overlooking the former woodyard, where wood chips are unloaded. It takes a handful of people to run the ultra-modern plant. The new Beloit paper machine is named "La Lièvre" for the river that was used to drive the logs in the days when the paper industry was a major employer.

In Kingston, where I live, Bell Canada has clear-cut the jobs of the telephone operators. The women are angry: not just because they once had jobs with union wages and benefits; not just because the company was stonewalling on its pay equity commitments; but also because it broke its promise to bring Nordia, its new contracted-out service, to town. Even though the jobs there would not have provided the same wages and benefits that the operators had enjoyed with CEP, they would have been jobs. Some former employees have found work at the new call centre. There's no union there.

All of this is, of course, nothing new to CEP, its members, activists, officers, and staff. The union has responded by following Max Michaud's advice about the need to organize. When I met Max he was feeling optimistic, and not just because of his union's historic breakthrough into the offshore oil industry at Hibernia. Max believed that organizing young, highly trained people in the technology sector would be an important challenge for the twenty-first-century CEP.

I also talked with Quebec and Newfoundland silvicultural workers, described by Martin Bedard of Local 3000Q, a man who has done his share of backbreaking work, as *"les enfants pauvres de la forêt,"* the poor children of the forest. These seasonal workers, many employed by heavy-handed contractors, are paid on a piece-rate basis for planting and thinning in rough terrain and all kinds of weather. I met the feisty women from Purdy's Chocolates, where they have won victory after victory against an anti-union factory owner. Many of these workers speak little English and were unsure about their rights. Then there was the remarkable K.H. Wong, fired for organizing Chinese-language newspaper workers who had never been in a union before. They spent seven weeks on a picket line to get a first contract. The CEP helped all of these people to organize.

Since its formation in 1992, CEP has organized over 35,000 new members. I did not get to meet the Calgary school board staff, the Winnipeg newspaper carriers, the Sarnia waste management workers, the toy makers at Wrebbit puzzle factory in suburban Montreal, the dairy workers in Vancouver, the truss and joist makers in Ste-Marthe-du-Cap, Quebec, or the people who pour the coffee at the donut shop in Espanola, Ont.

I did meet Clément L'Heureux, CEP's executive vice-president for Quebec, who expressed his belief that ten years of the new union boiled down to something quite simple – defending trade union principles. The servicing, the education, the organizing was familiar ground for CEP, a union that was changing with the times while at the same time sticking to its founding ideals.

"If I sit down and ask myself, 'What were the challenges that merger offered in 1992?' I must arrive at the conclusion that, 'Yes, we met the challenge and

MURRAY MOSHER

▲ *Executive vice-president, Quebec, Clément L'Heureux on the newly formed* CEP*: "We aren't here to rediscover fire, but rather to keep it burning."*

CEP secretary-treasurer ▲
André Foucault was impressed by the political maturity of unionists willing to grant a temporary dues surcharge, confident that it would be rescinded as soon as possible. And it was.

we will have to continue adapting in the future.' These changes are not for us, but for CEP members. They are the ones who have profited most from improved work conditions and higher salaries. This was our primary objective, well before the merger of the founding unions. We aren't here to rediscover fire, but rather to keep it burning."

Action and the meaning of solidarity

A BURN BARREL, some strikers joking among themselves, a handful of black-clad security guards: it all seemed pretty ordinary. The CEP's landmark strike at Lafarge Canada near Kingston was, however, exceptional. The first time I went to visit the picket line, in December 2001, I learned that the cement workers were on strike for less pay. They were represented by a union willing to back them all the way to force the multinational corporation to hire more workers instead of pushing the people in Local 219-O to put in exhausting overtime hours. Six months later the workers emerged victorious.

In the months that followed I learned that if this union wasn't reinventing the wheel, it was always ready to push it uphill against the biggest , and some of the most aggressive, employers. So the strike against the world's largest cement company wasn't that exceptional at all. In the ten years since the merger there had been no more combative union anywhere. CEP took on corporations like Abitibi-Consolidated, Bell, Fletcher Challenge, the CBC, Petro-Canada. It confronted rich, anti-union Canadians like Conrad Black and the Irvings. It didn't always win, but employers soon learned that it was a union that did not hesitate for a second to stand behind working people when they were under attack.

Ten years of the new ►
union boils down to something quite simple – defending trade union principles. Clément L'Heureux addresses a Quebec rally, May 2001.

At Westroc, just outside Montreal, I met three CEP activists whose local had been mauled in a strike in 1991, the year before the merger. When they walked out again nine years later, it was with a renewed sense of confidence and with $200 a week from the CEP Defense Fund – double what they got in 1991. When the employer made an offer four months into the strike, Local 134Q rejected it and held out for a better offer that came five months later. The CEP's feistiness was serving its members well.

During a period when Montreal drywall workers were walking the picket line, so too were thousands of other CEP members. Indeed, 34,563 members were on strike in the five-year period from 1996 to 2001. CEP secretary-treasurer André Foucault said, "During this period the Defense Fund paid out over $64.4 million. If we add to this the support received from special strike funds and responses to strike appeals, that amount climbs to well over $100 million."

But he was even more impressed by the political maturity that the young union displayed when the 1998 convention did not hesitate to grant permission for a temporary dues surcharge aimed at replenishing the strike fund. When the fund hit the $20 million mark, the union pledged that the surcharge would disappear; and that's what happened. It meant that the union could go to the well again if the costs of defending its members demanded it.

"The real significance of that is the credibility the organization gained with its membership," explained André. "We can go back to the membership and say, 'We need you to do a little extra, temporarily.' And they know we mean temporarily, because we said it once and proved that we meant it."

This sense of sticking together, known as solidarity, is the very basis of trade unionism. Even though the word was not always used, I noticed it again and again during my travels into CEP land.

In a Miramichi union hall, office worker Bonnie Galley described how getting a job at a unionized paper mill gave her a starting pay of $17 an hour instead of the $4.10 she had been getting as a hotel desk clerk in 1985. Even more, getting involved with the union and CEP's national women's committee, said Bonnie, helped her to develop social skills so that she was no longer intimidated when she spoke up at a meeting. At first she found it difficult to play a role in a male-dominated workplace. "Ten years ago when I had to come to a union meeting to speak, I used to shake in my boots," she recalled. "I don't anymore."

The local changed its by-laws so that the office workers, who are mainly women, automatically get representation on committees and on convention delegations. "We don't have to jump up and down and say 'Hey, we want to go too.' They know we're here and we're not going anywhere."

D. BOUZEK

▲ *"The union provides me with stability, benefits, and good wages. I had an obligation to give something back."*
• BONNIE GALLEY, MIRAMICHI, N.B.

*Marg Harbert, chair ▲
of the Women's
Committee, promotes
CEP'S Policy 913,
the comprehensive
Equality Action Plan.*

Bonnie's experience is reflected in the changes that CEP has introduced in order to promote equity issues. The 1998 convention passed Policy 913, the comprehensive Equality Action Plan, which committed the union to action promoting the rights and representation of women, people of colour, Aboriginal peoples, disabled people, and gays and lesbians. Urged on by activists like Mary Roberts, Marg Harbert, Ann Newman, and scores of others, a committee chaired by Brian Payne (then Western vice-president) worked to develop the new approach. The policy recognizes that racism, sexism, and other forms of discrimination exist in unions because they exist in society. As an organization committed to the struggle for a fairer society, the union decided that it had to promote equity issues internally.

Bonnie Galley has been part of that push. I asked her the same question I asked many of the CEP members I met. "It takes a lot of time. Why bother to get involved in the union, anyway?"

"The union does good things for me," she replied. "It provides me with stability and benefits and good wages. So I always kind of felt I had an obligation to give something back."

The need to give something back, the habit of solidarity, is deeply rooted not just in CEP but in the unions that came before it. I met Alain Leduc in the tiny windowless office that his local maintains in the corner of a giant appliance factory in east-end Montreal. It was the fiftieth anniversary of the former Communications Workers local. It was also the first anniversary of the start of the bitter strike of 2001. On the wall there was a poster from an international trade union conference of General Electric workers.

*Young and old, black ►
and white, men
and women: CEP
demonstrations are
inclusive. As an
organization committed
to the struggle for a
fairer society, the
union decided it had
to promote equity
issues internally.*

R. HATFIELD

Alain described how, for him, solidarity meant union members helping each other with literacy training, an area in which CEP has been a leader. Then there are members' personal issues, such as drug and alcohol problems. It also involved learning about the realities faced by workers in other industries. Having represented a dishwasher plant in a union of telephone operators and technicians, he was no stranger to an integrated union.

"The CEP is an open union and I don't think that ten years is very long," he said. "Of course we had to integrate all the components of the new union because their situations and histories were different. It wasn't automatic. We had to work at it."

His local neatly outmanoeuvred Camco when the company tried to bypass the union by sending scary letters to the members at home. The local set up its own website to communicate with the members during the strike. The members then sat back and watched while the company, whose top boss was being lionized by the business press for being such a smart fellow, scrambled to keep up. Alain was optimistic about how information technology would be able to help in the age-old task of worker organizing.

"Before long, most of our members will be on-line and that will be another way to reach them right at home," he said. "That will give us really significant opportunities, not just for our members, but non-unionized workers too."

Alain is clearly no Luddite, at least in the way that many people misunderstand the term. The Luddites were workers in nineteenth-century England who did not have any particular hostility to the machines they smashed, but rather to the employers using those machines in particular ways. This "collective bargaining by riot" has a long history, as workers have always found interesting ways of pressuring their employers. The Nottinghamshire Luddites, noted one historian of popular disturbances, "were using attacks on machinery as a means of coercing their employers into granting them concessions."

Another historian, more sympathetic to the Luddites, explained that Luddism was part of a movement to counter wage reduction. "Wrecking was simply a technique of trade unionism during the early phases of the industrial revolution," wrote Eric Hobsbawm in his 1952 essay "The Machine Breakers."

Hobsbawm was referring to a time when unions hardly even existed. The technique of sabotaging machines was not only a good way of making bosses pay attention, but also a way of ensuring solidarity among scattered, poorly paid men and women who had no strike funds but who could nevertheless organize effective, militant actions. In these actions, which the authorities called "riots," Hobsbawm saw the early roots of the core of worker

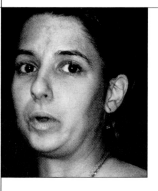

▲ *Colleen Manestar tells CEP delgates at the 1998 convention that equity-seeking groups want "a hand up, not a handout."*

organization. "The habit of solidarity, which is the foundation of effective trade unionism, takes time to learn. It takes even longer to become part of the unquestioned ethical code of the working class."

That phrase, "the habit of solidarity," reminds me of the man who first introduced me to this union. Don Holder had a way of persuading others by dint of his sheer enthusiasm. Don started out as a labourer in the Provincial Paper mill in Thorold, Ont., and went on to become a key architect of CEP. He wasn't very good with a prepared text, but any time he spoke from the heart you knew right away that he was someone you had to listen to. Not long before his death he travelled back to Thorold to support CEP members who were occupying the old mill, trying to save it from closing. Don had the habit of solidarity.

I noticed that this foundation was certainly established in the new union he helped to found: not just in the commitment to a solid Defense Fund, or in the members who volunteered so much time to support their union; but also in what led CEP to decide at its first regular convention in 1994 that the struggle for shorter hours should be a top priority. The movement for shorter working hours is as old as the trade union movement. Shorter hours not only create more time for the members, but also promote more jobs for other workers. The decision to continue this radical social agenda was simply part of this Habit of Solidarity.

Don Holder had the "habit of solidarity". CEP's founding president died in 2001.

CHAPTER ONE

MURRAY MOSHER

A few days in May, Part 1:
FORT McMURRAY

THIS BOOK IS THE PRODUCT of a series of visits to places where the CEP is active. I could also have gone to Winnipeg or Alma or Smooth Rock Falls, but there's only so much you can cover when trying to find out about an organization that represents so many different workers in so many places in such a large country. My travels started in the east with a trip to Grand Falls, Nfld., and finished with a visit to Regina by way of the Alberta oil sands.

I spent May Day in Fort McMurray, Alta., a small city that's getting much bigger. People there are in the middle of a $27 billion oil boom. At a time when many towns across the country are desperately trying to boost employment by competing for call centres, Fort McMurray has so much growth, at least in one sector, that newcomers have trouble finding a place to live. The Chamber of Commerce wrings its hands about service-sector labour shortages. They have

▲ *Presents of the founding unions: Reg Basken (ECWU), Don Holder (CPU), Fred Pomeroy (CWC). The formation of CEP meant that a new union, one of Canada's biggest, immediately loomed large on the labour landscape.*

11

to pay fast-food workers more than Alberta's minimum wage.

When you pass the Boomtown Casino and cross the bridge over the Athabaska River, you go onto a new divided highway that climbs to the thriving suburbs of Thickwood and Dickenson, where old houses are the ones that date from the 1970s. Moving vans are backed up to unfinished houses next door to places where anxious developers are using industrial-strength hot-air blowers to dry the freshly poured basements. Signs for Wood Buffalo Estates and Lindal Cedar Homes are everywhere.

In other tracts of land the boreal forest has been stripped away, to be replaced by rows of mobile homes on tiny lots. "They call them 'manufactured homes' now," explained the millwright acting as my tour guide. Since he arrived from Newfoundland over twenty years ago, Keith Barrington had seen a lot of change – and lived in a lot of different houses. He became as familiar with the local real estate scene as he once was with the spaghetti-like network of roads at Suncor's Steepbank Mining Complex down the Athabaska River –

the place where they mine the molasses-like oil sand.

Keith, the former president of CEP Local 707, is now the union rep for the area. "That place would sell for $400,000," he told me, pointing to a sprawling new house with a three-car garage. "The manufactured homes go for $170,000."

The Toronto-level prices don't deter members of Local 707. A Suncor operator who hit town when Keith did and subsequently bought and sold a couple of houses could now easily afford the place with all that garage space. Though he preferred running marathons to snowmobiling, Keith said that many oil workers needed lots of room. In Fort McMurray (simply "McMurray" to the locals) a union electrician at Suncor can make more than one of the oil company's professional engineers.

"There's a massive amount of toys here. Quads, Ski-Doos, Harleys. There are even special lots where you can park your RV."

... continued on page 17

◀ *Merger Committee, Canadian Paperworkers Union, Communications and Electrical Workers of Canada, Energy and Chemical Workers Union, September 1992.*

BACK ROW FROM LEFT: *Claude Groulx (CPU), Jo-Anne Swayze (CPU), Ronald Beaton (CPU), Yvan Bélanger (CPU), Willie Desbiens (CPU, secretary-treasurer).*

MIDDLE ROW FROM LEFT: *Robert Pelletier (CWC), Henri Gauthier (ECWU), Ralph Wyatt (CWC, secretary-treasurer), Linda MacKenzie-Nicholas (CWC), Randy Billow (CPU), Jean-François Primeau (ECWU), Dawn van Nostrand (ECWU), Gordon Steininger (ECWU).*

FRONT ROW FROM LEFT: *Fred Pomeroy (CWC, president), Don Holder (CPU, president), Reg Basken (ECWU, president).*

From a trattoria to a consensus

THEY WERE SIXTEEN PEOPLE who knew they had a job to do, but it wasn't happening. There was a lot of wheel spinning but no traction – even though they were all convinced that their own organizations had reached a plateau and weren't growing, that a new organization offered fresh opportunities.

"Like most things in the union movement it took a long time to put together," said Fred Pomeroy, the leader of the Communications and Electrical Workers of Canada (CWC) in 1991, when all of this was happening.

The talks involved the CWC, the Energy and Chemical Workers Union (ECWU), led by Reg Basken, and the Canadian Paperworkers Union (CPU), led by Don Holder. They were held at the Canadian Paperworkers' headquarters, a magnificent old building once occupied by Montreal's anglophone captains of industry when St. James Street was the bastion of Canadian capitalism. Fred Pomeroy came up with three other figures of speech – from poker, knitting, and war – to describe the first set of negotiations that gave rise to the CEP.

"People were keeping their cards close to their chest."

"We were knitting one and purling two and not making much progress."

"People were reluctant to stick their foot into no man's land on an issue."

Dawn van Nostrand attended the meetings as a rank and file member of the ECWU. She said, "It was like the scene from *Star Trek* where the Federation and the Klingons are meeting for the first time."

There were a lot of issues, many of them contentious. What would the dues structure of the union be? Where would it be based? Would there be regional or provincial councils? Who would get what job? What about the makeup of the executive board? Setting up a new union was a thorny business, like writing the constitution of a new country. In 1991 Fred was the only one with a laptop. The screen showed a handful of issues that had been resolved and dozens outstanding.

Someone finally suggested that instead of heading their separate ways, the frustrated trade unionists should all go out to dinner together. Someone else knew of a good Italian place. Many plates of pasta and nearly as many bottles of Chianti later something had happened.

Randy Billow, a millwright from a New Westminster, B.C., paper mill, said that Willie Desbiens of the CPU had been singing with such enthusiasm that evening that the kitchen staff came out to listen. It had all started when the owner of the place, who was quite a singer himself, started to serenade the group. He was

As time passed, more and more of the new union's activists got to know each other on picket lines, at educational sessions, at labour councils.

quickly joined by Willie and another veteran, CWC secretary-treasurer Ralph Wyatt. Pretty soon everyone was having a rollicking good time. Something had clicked.

"The skids were greased after that," Fred recalled.

The discussions that opened up were peppered with the debates and arguments that are vital ingredients in this kind of undertaking. When things got too heated, Ralph Wyatt, one of the elder statesmen, would lean back, a two-inch ash drooping from his cigarette (you were still allowed to smoke inside back then), and smooth things out. Ralph, who had started out as a telephone switchman in 1946, had a way of providing just enough context to put the issue into perspective.

"Things were changing," recalled Ralph. "It didn't matter which sector you were in, there was not going to be the same number of employees. If we wanted to have some say in what was going on, we had to expand somehow."

The issue of having a say was not just important in dealing with employers who were getting bigger all the time, that were merging and consolidating. It also played out within the broader labour movement, with unions all around them getting bigger all the time. Ironically, Fred Pomeroy and the CPU's Don Holder had first talked about the possibility of merging at the Canadian Auto Workers' Port Elgin centre, where they were attending a Canadian Labour Congress executive meeting.

▲ *Willie Desbiens leads the Founding Convention in "Solidarity Forever."*

The merger committee, made up of both rank and file and executive members of CEP's founding unions, held a series of discussions before taking their show on the road to sell the deal they had hammered out. It wasn't too hard a job, because most of the members who attended the information meetings understood the current realities of union and workplace. The workforces in the central offices of the phone companies, in pulp and paper mills, and in chemical plants and oil refineries were being eroded by technological change and downsizing.

Unemployment was stubbornly high, with the country in the middle of a deep depression. Not only that, the labour movement was going through a structural transformation, with good manufacturing jobs being hollowed out of the middle. More and more people were working longer hours in smaller workplaces that were harder and more expensive to organize. More people were working at temporary, part-time, and contract jobs. Employers took advantage of all the changes – many of which were of their own making – posing stiff challenges even to the largest trade unions.

Not everyone at the information meetings was happy. (At what union meeting is everyone ▶

happy?) On one occasion Randy Billow, who attended sessions with energy and communications locals, found himself in Pincher Creek, in southwestern Alberta not far from the B.C. border. One of the workers from the Shell facility there began to complain that he had heard all about the B.C. paperworkers. They were totally anti-company and were always out on strike.

Randy told how one of the ECWU rank and file members jumped up to the mike and said, "I work with those people on labour councils. Just because they have draconian employers doesn't mean they're the go-on-strike-anytime idiots that you're portraying. They're good people."

Less than a year after the pasta dinner, the founding unions held three separate mini-conventions in Montreal. After these meetings ratified a merger agreement (96 per cent in the CWC, 90.5 per cent in the ECWU, and 83 per cent in the CPU) they got together for the new CEP's founding convention. The first president elected was Don Holder of the CPU, a natural leader. One of his main assets was his sheer enthusiasm, which translated into a lively warmth. Don had a knack for getting people to listen when he talked, even though he had a unique way of torturing the English language into "Holderisms." Don died in 2001 at the age of sixty-six.

Randy Billow recalled the emotion he experienced when the merger committee followed a bagpiper into a room where twelve hundred delegates waited.

▲ *CEP founding president Don Holder, whose infectious enthusiasm played a big part in the birth of the new union.*

"When we turned the corner and I saw that crowd, I had tears running down my face," he said. "When it was all over I cried like a baby. I was emotionally drained."

Ten years later the jelling process at CEP continues. Distinct cultures still separate off some of the people who recall the old days when conventions were smaller and you had a lot in common with people who did the same kind of work. But as time passed, more and more of the new union's activists got to know each other on picket lines, at educational sessions, at labour councils. They met on protest marches, at demonstrations, and at women's and regional conferences. They gradually melded into a single organization of people who realize that what they have in common far outweighs any of their differences.

"We were knitting one and purling two and not making much progress."

In addition to a 12.5 per cent wage increase in the latest three-year contract, CEP members at Suncor recently got a $25,000 bonus when they helped cut the cost of producing a barrel of oil. The company slogan was "$10 by '02," meaning that it was costing Suncor $10 to transform two tonnes of sticky grit called bitumen into a barrel of oil using high pressure, naphtha, superheated steam, filters, spinners. The process also uses some of the world's biggest trucks, massive amounts of water, and lots of energy to produce energy. Together, Suncor and its non-union rival Syncrude produce half of Canada's oil. Within twenty-five years some of the world's biggest corporations (Shell planned to open a new mine by the end of 2002) will be pumping 70 per cent of the nation's oil from the Fort McMurray area.

As we headed back downtown to the CEP office we passed a gas station. I noticed that the price was 72.5 cents a litre. "Just because you're in oil country doesn't mean that you're going to get cheap gas," Keith said, with a laugh.

This oil country was not exactly union-friendly territory. The Alberta Conservatives had passed labour laws that made it hard to organize. But that had not stopped Local 707. It now represented callers and cashiers at the Bingo Palace as well as workers at Transwest, a Suncor contractor. Three weeks after the local signed some seventy workers at Greenlight, a company that held Suncor's cleaning contract, the firm lost the contract to the non-union Best

> "Just because you're in oil country doesn't mean that you're going to get cheap gas," Keith said, with a laugh.

Although they may not head for a trattoria to join the owner in a chorus of an old Frank Sinatra tune, they are a group that has learned to work and even play together.

The way it had all turned out was perhaps best summed up in the reflections of Marc Caron from the venerable Belgo paper mill in Shawinigan, Quebec. Marc said that for him the merger was "traumatizing." At the time he believed that it was a step back, and he still leans that way. In the old days the big meetings were devoted to discussions of the issues faced by workers in paper mills.

"We were always on the same wavelength. Today's meetings are not like that."

Marc had spent thirty years at the mill and almost as many as a union activist when he said that. He paused before going on to acknowledge that he was one of the "old wolves."

"We got used to our daily routine with all the people we knew," he added. "Losing that overnight wasn't easy. I remain convinced that, in the end, there is something to gain from having done this, and everyone will benefit from it." △

Fort McMurray. ▶
The tires on a giant
Suncor truck weigh in
at five tonnes. The workers
at Canada's first oil
sands plant, represented
by CEP, enjoy some of
the best wages and
working conditions in
the energy sector.

Facilities Services. Many of the CEP members lost their jobs, but caught on with Best. The link between the organizing campaign and the loss of the contract was uncertain, but Keith Barrington figured that Suncor management was not exactly pleased about their contract workers getting together with the union that represented fifteen hundred regular workers.

Within a year CEP had organized the Best workers too. Before they signed cards Keith made sure that he reminded them of the possible connection between their previous organizing drive and losing their jobs. The response he got was one of the most rewarding of his years as a union activist. "We don't care," they told him. "We need the support of a union. We want CEP."

Apparently the cleaners remembered that their collective agreement at Greenlight had included new money and better working conditions. Suncor subsequently signed a new three-year agreement with Best Services. By 2002 CEP had ten thousand members in Alberta.

The spacious offices of Local 707 occupied a conspicuous spot on Franklin Avenue, Fort McMurray's main street. On the wall of the boardroom – which a lot of other unions use for meetings – were dozens of photos – ringette teams, hockey teams, softball teams – all sponsored by CEP, the dominant union in town, a union that takes its local responsibilities seriously.

Heartbreak and the two-way street

BEFORE HEADING OFF from Fort McMurray to Regina I visited the Suncor Energy mine site, where the fifteen hundred or so CEP members work as machine operators or in other skilled trades. The thing that always strikes visitors is the fantastic scale of the place. Some of the trucks that trundle along roads with names like Extraction Way are older Komatsu Haulpaks. Some are the newer Caterpillar 979s. These vehicles are overwhelmingly huge. Their tires alone weigh in at five tonnes and cost $45,000 each. For the operators, climbing up to work is like going upstairs to the top of a three-storey house. There are supposedly a trillion or more barrels of oil out there in the Fort McMurray area – 300 billion of them recoverable. So it's not surprising that Suncor could label its Borealis Lodge, temporary accommodation for the five thousand workers on its multi-billion-dollar expansion, the largest hotel in the country. Indeed, everything about the place screams "BIG!"

At least that's the main impression the tourists come away with, and that's what I felt, too. But since my tour guides were trade unionists, I learned about a side of the place that the official tours don't emphasize. Roland Lefort, my guide on day two – May Day – explained that the regular reports of what sounded like gunfire were propane cannons fired to scare birds away from the

Since my tour guides were trade unionists, I learned about a side of the place that the official tours don't emphasize. Roland Lefort … explained that the regular reports of what sounded like gunfire were propane cannons fired to scare birds away from the toxic tailing ponds.

Despite all the money and the prosperity and the jobs and the high-priced toys, some people were still being left behind. There is still poverty and joblessness in Fort McMurray.

toxic tailing ponds. But these were lakes, not ponds. When one came into sight I noticed that the ominous-looking surface was dotted with little scarecrow figures bobbing on empty drums: another way of trying to keep the birds from the poisons in the water. The liquid waste, Rollie said, was "the heartbreak of the whole operation."

Rollie, a Cape Breton Acadian and secretary-treasurer of Local 707, explained that the leadership of the local was forged by a bitter five-month strike in 1986. A lot had changed since then. The Suncor workers had belonged to an independent union but joined the Energy and Chemical Workers after the strike. They became part of the CEP with the 1992 merger and watched their numbers double in the years since. They now make up one of the biggest bargaining units in the union, and as such are big contributors to the strength-in-numbers thinking that underpinned the merger. For Rollie, it's a two-way street.

"The national office gives us a sense of direction," he said, emphasizing the importance of national union policy when workers are confronted by corporate scare tactics. (The oil sands operation is the fourth-largest producer of carbon dioxide in Canada.) "It's good to have the national telling us it's important to support the Kyoto Accord even though we're in the oil industry."

Part of my Fort McMurray tour took me to a place that most tourists don't visit. It was a place where you couldn't get your picture taken beside a giant tire, but where they would help you out if you were having trouble feeding your family. The Fort McMurray Food Bank was across the street from a transmission shop in an industrial park on the way to the airport. The

CEP, the dominant ► *union in town, takes its community responsibilities seriously. Former Local 707 presidents Walter Manning and Brian Campbell.*

nondescript building served as the union office during the landmark Suncor strike in 1986.

"The union is a really big supporter of the food bank, especially during our December food drive," staffer Carol Castor explained. "I don't know what this place would do without them. Rollie's our main man when it comes to getting stuff."

She and volunteer Tracy Hickey showed me around the little warehouse, its homemade plywood shelves stuffed with Betty Crocker Supreme Brownie mix, soup, flour, and more. One little room was devoted to toilet paper and tissues, and a big, seven-door cooler bulged with eggs and fresh produce. The boomtown food bank faced the usual challenges; there was too much pasta and Kraft dinner, not enough tuna and peanut butter. Rollie Lefort followed along, clearly proud of the place. He served on the board and co-ordinated the big pre-Christmas blitz. It was no problem when they had to rebuild the compressor in the cooler because there was lots of skilled labour around.

Tracy Hickey told me how she put in a lot of hours from November to February, preparing for the food drive and organizing the resulting inventory. Tracy had a simple explanation for why she spent so much time at the food bank. "I wanted to be involved with something that's community-based."

The Canadian Union of Postal Workers, also represented on the food bank board, used to collect food directly from Fort McMurray households in what the posties jokingly referred to as the "Break My Back" campaign. The letter carriers would leave pamphlets urging people to put food items at the door for collection. For the next few days the workers would be weighed down with groceries as they went around on their routes. Eventually the loads got to be too heavy for the letter carriers, and the collection ended in 1992.

"I guess the post office is like a lot of other union workplaces, " I remarked. "Not too many young people there." Rollie and the two women laughed in agreement, but pointed out that the take from the December food drive had jumped from two to eighteen tonnes in a few short years. It also pulled in $50,000, added Carol.

Fort McMurray has to be one of the few cities in Canada where, rather than closing branches, the big banks are actually opening bigger ones. Keith had explained that the people in the thriving oil capital lived in a different world altogether. "We only read about recession in the paper."

Yet despite the differences, some things up there seemed the same. Despite all the money and the prosperity and the jobs and the high-priced toys, some people were still being left behind. There is still poverty and joblessness in Fort McMurray. Service jobs may pay more than minimum wage, but the cost of

Rollie Lefort, a Cape Breton Acadian and secretary-treasurer of Local 707, explained that the leadership of the local was forged by a bitter five-month strike in 1986. A lot had changed since then.

living has gone through the roof. People fall through the cracks because prosperity is unequally distributed, particularly when governments are made up of nodding yes-men for the petroleum industry. With Alberta's Tory cabinet ministers free to speculate in oil and gas companies that they are supposed to regulate, the "oil patch" was blessed with the lowest royalty rates in thirty years just as public health and education budgets were being cut to the bone. For its part, Ottawa's generosity to the oil industry meant that the government had written off $2.8 billion in loans and benefits to non-renewable energy projects. This did not include federal tax breaks for the oil sands, which could cost everyone – including food bank users – up to $2 billion.

"Here in McMurray we have a beautiful history of unions working for the common good," Rollie said as we headed downtown. He had chaired the recent United Way campaign, and the fundraising effort at Suncor, he said, raised as much money as the campaign at the non-union Syncrude operation, where twice as many people work. He was proud of what his union and others had been able to do, both on the job and off. The union made "a difference" in the town, he told me.

"Not just by the high wages we've negotiated and the hockey teams we support, but by protecting social rights. I make sure that people know that I'm doing my volunteer work as a union person."

CHAPTER TWO

The battle for Hibernia

WHEN THEY DECIDED to fire Daisy Parsons they phoned to ask her to come in to discuss a "restructuring" program. They hired a counsellor to ask her how she felt. They had a big brown envelope containing The Package. They offered to put her up in a hotel or hire a taxi to take her home. They seemed confident about what was best for her.

Daisy didn't agree. She figured then and there that she could make up her own mind about The Package, even though she recalled feeling dazed about the whole thing at the time. They had, after all, been telling everyone that they were all part of the Hibernia family. If you needed a letter to take to the bank for your mortgage, no problem – you would be able to pay off that new home because the jobs were so secure. If you gave 110 per cent, things were fine. There was a lot of oil. Hibernia was, after all, going to be a pioneer of offshore excellence.

"Get out of my way!" snapped Daisy. "I have to have my own space to figure out what's going on here."

▲ *The Hibernia platform lies 135 kilometres southeast of St. John's in the frigid waters of the North Atlantic. "You could stand outside with a bunch of flyers, but you'd better know how to bob quite successfully."*
• RAY CLUNEY

Hibernia promised jobs ▶ *to a province that suffered the worst unemployment in the country. In February 1996, CEP members in Grand Falls, Nfld., marched to save Unemployment Insurance.*

"It's a wonder the CEP doesn't get fed up with all this and just walk away."

After she returned home to Southern Harbour on Placentia Bay, she and her husband Brian tried to figure out what to do. It wasn't easy. They had decided that the security of Daisy's new job in the offshore meant that he could sell his old fishing boat and buy a new one. Lorna Ryan, whose husband Denis had worked on the ill-fated *Ocean Ranger*, recalled that when word of the new job came in, "We could hardly believe our good luck."

Daisy and Brian had felt the same way. But things had gone sour. The Package was tempting and at first Brian felt that she should make the best of the situation and walk away with the money that was on the table. Voices were sometimes raised. Daisy described the situation delicately. "It put a lot of stress on my marriage."

"There's no way you can fight it alone," Brian said. "This company is too big. You just have to face the facts."

Daisy, who described herself as a bit of a fighter, would not budge. "I just stood fast to what I believed in. Then when the CEP stepped in and said they were going to fight for us, Brian became more comfortable."

So her husband kept on taking the *JSN Explorer* out on the water, looking for crab and scallops and cod and lobster. Daisy kept on going to the meetings and the hearings, with Brian sitting in on the discussions. Two years later he was often saying to Daisy, "It's a wonder the CEP doesn't get fed up with all this and just walk away."

It doesn't. And it hasn't.

Against all odds

ACCORDING TO RAY CLUNEY, he's a bit of an organizer and, for the past few years, a little bit of a papermaker. Like many Newfoundlanders, he has a way with words. He is also a shrewd observer of both the world around him and the people who live there. It all helped him make a contribution to the first successful campaign to organize an offshore oil platform in North America.

"The most dependable thing in the world is greed," Ray told me. "Greed lives in all of us. Once they got first oil, it became 'Let's trim to the bone.'"

Ray lives in Grand Falls. For thirty years he has been working at a mill that was once one of the biggest in the world and is still among the oldest in the country. The mill was opened in 1906, its eight paper machines financed by an English press baron worried about how political instability might set back his traditional Baltic sources of wood fibre. Lord Northcliffe had no worries in Newfoundland, where the government eagerly gave him access to the forests. He never had to pay a penny for the wood. Nothing. Rivers like the Gander, the Humber, the White Bear, and the Exploits provided handy highways for pulpwood, and the Exploits supplied cheap power for the mill.

I met with Ray in the sprawling bingo parlour that the union uses for meetings of the local. The union hall is known to people in Grand Falls as Club 63, named for one of the locals at the mill. It's a social centre. The little offices housing locals 59N, 60N, 63, and 88 are across from the bingo hall and there's a smoky bar downstairs. It has taken CEP locals five years – and counting – to organize the Hibernia oil platform, 317 kilometres offshore in the North Atlantic Ocean, and the campaign was run out of Club 63 and the Holiday Inn in St. John's.

The organizing campaign was, and is, a big challenge, Ray told me. They have been up against the paternalism and manic anti-union attitude of multinational oil companies bigger than most countries – a consortium including Exxon-Mobil and others. The employers erected costly legal barricades whenever they got a chance. Most organizers face these kinds of obstacles, but at least they can go to the worksite to meet the workers. In this case, Ray couldn't just grab a handful of leaflets, hop in his car, and head for the plant gate. The Hibernia employees go to work in helicopters; and they report to the job not five days a week but eight times a year, twenty-one days at a time.

"You could stand outside with a bunch of flyers, but you'd better know how to bob quite successfully," Ray said with a broad smile.

CEP's against-all-odds campaign combined the Newfoundland experience of Ray Cluney and national representative Ron Smith – both of whom came out of the Grand Falls mill – with the understanding of the oil business of Brian Campbell and Keith Kleinwachter, both of whom had spent years in the energy industry. The organizing drive also enjoyed a little bit of luck, at least at

Ray couldn't just grab a handful of leaflets, hop in his car, and head for the plant gate. The Hibernia employees go to work in helicopters; and they report to the job not five days a week but eight times a year, twenty-one days at a time.

Keith Kleinwachter joined the Hibernia campaign in November 1998. Brother Kleinwachter passed away in 2002.

first. When the Hibernia Management and Development Corporation sent its information on the design and safety of the rig to the concerned parties at the safety hearings, the consortium left the employee list in the binder.

"We promptly returned it," CEP rep Ron Smith said. "It just passed through the copier first."

From then on, though, it was hard slogging. Despite their photocopying, the organizers never had an accurate employee list. They had to make phone calls and follow-up visits to scattered employees who easily make $90,000 a year, who were being assured that they all had secure jobs with the Hibernia family. The workers lived in the equivalent of a very pleasant hotel where women like Daisy Parsons prepared sumptuous meals and cleaned their rooms. After each long hitch on the rig they might hurry home to New Glasgow, Nova Scotia, or Glasgow, Scotland. When you did succeed in reaching them at home, they might just not feel like discussing life on a job far out in the storm-swept ocean.

Even though most Hibernia workers live in Newfoundland, it's a big province. This meant lots of trips on icy roads to Birchy Bay or Pouch Cove. CEP organizers "from away" sometimes thought they had commitments to sign cards just because people who sounded interested on the phone were hospitable on the doorstep and invited them in for tea. But they didn't necessarily sign up. Newfoundlanders are friendly folk.

"In Ontario if they're not interested they're going to tell you in very blunt words," said Ron Smith. "But they won't do that in Newfoundland."

Then there was what Ray Cluney described as "the fear factor." Good organizers like Ray have to be amateur psychologists who can figure people out and quickly establish trust. "They have to know they can count on what you say being real," Ray explained. "You have to make sure they know," he said, "that 'My first concern is you, my second concern is the campaign.' You can't just say it, you've got to mean it. You've got to have them believe it."

Ray often successfully made other Newfoundlanders feel comfortable with the idea of talking union. Once he got that far, he had to overcome the culture of secrecy and security promoted by employers in the offshore. Some people were worried about meeting them at home, insisting on furtive rendezvous at the local Tim Hortons.

"Hibernia? You swear to God it's James Bond again. These guys really think they are living in Los Alamos creating Fat Boy, that first atomic bomb. They're legends in their own minds."

Because a union card only has a ninety-day life in Newfoundland, CEP organizers were always having to re-sign supporters. Then there was the rival union that, as all the organizers put it, let the CEP pave the road so they could drive over it. This resulted in confusion among a workforce that was already polarized on the question of unionization. In November 1999, when the competing union, the Fish Food and Allied Workers/CAW applied to the provincial labour board for certification, CEP was forced to do the same even though the organizers did not believe they were quite ready. They figured that they could ill afford to have a formal vote in which the only name on the ballot was that of their rival. In December two separate votes, one for FFAW/CAW and one for CEP Local 97, were held concurrently on the same platform. The voting continued ashore and then by mail into the new year. But after much wrangling, and over a year later, at the end of March 2001, the labour board ruled that neither union had the necessary percentage of signed cards required for the ballots to be counted. Both unions lost out, with CEP falling short by a heartbreaking four cards.

No one had ever predicted that it would be easy to organize the offshore. But CEP knew this was its jurisdiction and that, if it were successful in organizing Hibernia and the other east-coast projects that were in the pipeline, it would be the unchallenged union in the sector. Other drives would be easier because, like any other group of workers, the women and men on the rigs form a community. They talk to each other, and word of an effective union offering solid service would be bound to spread. Still, there were a few I-told-you-so voices, even within CEP ranks. Hadn't the energy industry veterans west of the Atlantic region warned the Newfoundlanders about the cash-rich oil companies that had once lamely justified their lucrative tax breaks by saying that exploration was a "big, tough, expensive job"?

No one in Newfoundland who applied for a job on an oil rig during the optimistic boom that continued after the Ocean Ranger disaster was unaware of the fate of those who worked on that platform.

◄ *Because a union card only has a ninety-day life in Newfoundland, CEP organizers were always having to re-sign supporters. Brian Campbell, Ray Cluney and Harold Hawco with the precious Hibernia cards.*

The same could be said about the task of organizing those companies. Even though Ed Nelson, CEP secretary-treasurer at the time, had warned Atlantic vice-president Elmo Whittom that it would take about five years to crack the offshore, CEP locals in Newfoundland did not hesitate to press ahead. When it was all over, one of the organizers remarked that the campaign had indeed taken longer than the First World War.

"The budget was just about the same," quipped another.

Labour history, island culture, and legal wrangling

TWO HUGE CHAPTERS in Newfoundland history loomed over CEP's dogged fight for the rights of offshore workers.

One was the *Ocean Ranger* disaster of 1982, when fifty-six Newfoundlanders and twenty-six others died needlessly. It was the result, according to the subsequent royal commission inquiry, of poor design and inadequate – and unenforced – government regulations. What's more, the commission concluded that the *Ocean Ranger*'s corporate operators – including Mobil – failed to provide adequate safety training and survival suits. They also failed to equip standby vessels with proper rescue equipment. A family member of one victim provided a bitter assessment of what happened after the wild storm slashed across Newfoundland on Valentine's Day, 1982: "I couldn't care less about the offshore now. It will only mean more money for Mobil and the other oil companies…. A man is nothing to an oil company, he's only a number."

The island culture is moulded by the lure and lore of an often-bountiful, often unforgiving ocean where the ice and the fog and the gales have meant,

Organizing requires a long-term commitment of money and people, and the willingness to follow up. In January 1995, CEP held an organizing school in Western Canada for locals that had recently joined.

more often than not, that there are no coffins. But as with the open boats of the inshore fishery, the elaborate nautical fortresses are still subject to North Atlantic storms that are becoming nastier and more frequent as global climate chaos accelerates. No one in Newfoundland who applied for a job on an oil rig during the optimistic boom that continued after the *Ocean Ranger* disaster was unaware of the fate of those who worked on that platform. The corporations and the government had been stung by the widespread knowledge that so many had died as a result of their negligence. All of which helped to account for the new emphasis that Hibernia's owners placed on safety training and equipment. (Ray Cluney had to learn how to escape from an upside-down simulated helicopter at the bottom of a swimming pool before being allowed to travel to the Hibernia platform.)

The other milestone in Newfoundland labour history unfolded among the trees behind the shore. When Ray was a teenager who hadn't yet started as a papermaker in Grand Falls, the men who supplied the mill with pulpwood were paid $1.05 an hour. The supply of workers was far greater than the supply of jobs. The pulp wood cutters washed in cold, scummy water slopping around the open barrels outside the tarpaper shacks where they slept. The owners of the Anglo-Newfoundland Development Company at Grand Falls and Joey Smallwood's government in St. John's had no reason to alter the long-standing status quo. But the loggers and the upstart International Woodworkers union did, and in 1959 they launched a bitter wintertime strike that resulted in battles with scabs, multiple arrests, and the death of one Mountie. The tone had been set after the loggers voted 98.8 per cent in favour of a strike. The last meeting before the walkout took place at the Anglo-Newfoundland Development Company office in Grand Falls. The union asked if there were any terms the company would accept. "Yes, if you'll take a pay cut."

In the end the strike fizzled after Smallwood's government rammed through a law that the premier's biographer called "the most punitive anti-labour legislation of any post-war Canadian government other than that of Duplessis." As with the *Ocean Ranger* disaster, there was a royal commission that got to the heart of the matter: too many desperately poor loggers so anxious for jobs that they could be forced to live in "hovels which would not be used for hen-houses except by the most primitive farmer." In a bit of delicious irony, it was the legacy of Smallwood's labour legislation that helped CEP to organize Hibernia successfully.

Looking back, Ron Smith figured that there was a culture clash between the Newfoundlanders and some of the Americans who had a high-handed way of doing things.

GREG LOCKE

The worker who was ▶ *guilty of diabetes was on the next helicopter out. This happened in the middle of one of the organizing drives, and when CEP retained a lawyer and began to holler about human rights, the fellow got his job back.*

In 2000, after Local 97's narrow four-card shortfall, CEP and FFAW/CAW were faced with a provincial law banning another organizing drive for six months. The bar on organizing prompted the rival union to shrug its shoulders, but CEP organizers went back to the province's labour history. Smallwood, obsessed with "outside" (read: national or international) unions, had passed a labour law that gave recognition to individual locals only, not to central trade union organizations. The CEP had set up a separate organization, Local 97, to conduct its initial sign-up drive. Why not simply reapply under a different local? In another bit of irony, the unionists chose Local 60N, the CEP local representing loggers.

"We applied under Local 60N and we launched a new campaign," said Ray Cluney, whose own papermakers Local 88 is just down the hall from Local 60. "We went to the labour board. The lawyer for the FFAW/CAW said we were out to lunch. The oil industry said, 'They'll never win that.' The labour board, however, had a different opinion."

The labour board decision gave CEP a clear field. Meanwhile, the employer lent a helping hand. As veteran organizers know, their best friends are employers who give workers who might previously have been opposed to signing a card good reasons to consider the need for union protection. In short, the employer is often as helpful to an organizer as an up-to-date list of the workforce or a handful of energetic union supporters on the job. In the case of Hibernia, once the first oil started flowing, some of the front-line management were "the best kind of SOBs a union organizer could ever want."

One of the issues was favouritism. Bosses who discriminate between people they like and those with what they see as bad attitudes have always irritated workers. If there's anything more annoying than watching someone suck up to a supervisor, it's having a boss who plays the game. Once that starts to happen, it gives new meaning to employer talk about the workplace being one big family.

Another issue was managers who arrived in Newfoundland with "attitude." One Texas oilman opened a fridge and noticed a vial of insulin. He asked angrily what it was doing there.

Apparently one of the workers was a diabetic. "He keeps those all over the platform for safety reasons," someone told the Texan.

"Fire him! We don't have diabetics in the oil industry."

The worker who was guilty of diabetes was on the next helicopter out. This happened in the middle of one of the organizing drives, but when CEP retained a lawyer and began to holler about human rights, the fellow got his job back. Looking back, Ron Smith figured that there was a culture clash between the Newfoundlanders and some of the Americans who had a high-handed way of doing things.

Hibernia management also brought in a job evaluation scheme they called a personal development program. What it meant was that two millwrights working side by side could be getting different rates of pay because a supervisor gave one a better review than the other. Sometimes the difference amounted to $5,000 for the same work. The old question "Is that fair?" came into play, just as it did when people began to notice that they were being paid differently for the same job just because they were hired at a different time.

The way Daisy Parsons remembers it, morale was pretty good on the Hibernia platform while things were getting established. The company was generous with bonuses, gifts, and prizes as it hurried to get "first oil" flowing. Even after that, things were alright, although the pace of work and long hours proved a deadening grind. There was no overtime pay, and working fifteen hours a day during punishing twenty-one-day shifts takes its toll. Yet no matter how hard she worked on her regular job and or the extra hours she put in as a member of the medical response team, it didn't seem to matter.

"When it came time for promotions, if you weren't in with the supervisors, or you weren't related to somebody, you were going to stay where you were," she recalled. "I would never want a union offshore for the sake of the money or the benefits. That's very good. But it's the security of your job. It's having a voice and having seniority, because if someone doesn't like you, too bad. You can be replaced."

And replaced she was.

D. BOUZEK

▲ *Morale was pretty good on the Hibernia platform while things were getting established. Daisy Parsons in interview with author Jamie Swift.*

"If you're going to ▲
organize people, you
don't just turn your back
on them." Brian Payne
meets with one of the
twenty-five laid-off
Hibernia workers.

Daisy figures that the main reason she was fired was because she had started to speak out about what she felt was wrong on the job. In the paternalistic oil business, workers who do this sort of thing do not exactly curry favour with the boss. She told management that she knew they were anxious to keep the union out, but that unless the growing list of complaints about favouritism and hours and arrogance was taken seriously, it was just making the job of the organizers easier. The company was disregarding the old saying, "Abuse a man unjustly, and you will make friends for him."

On February 17, 2000, Hibernia Management and Development Corporation brought in their counsellors and prepared their packages and laid off Daisy and twenty-four other workers. Perhaps it was because some of them had signed union cards. Maybe it was just another step in pioneering offshore excellence. Or maybe it was a straight downsizing manoeuvre. Whatever the case, it did nothing to stop the organizing drive as the remaining workers started to add "Who's next?" to the old question "Is that fair?" Indeed, the second campaign under Local 60 that began fifteen months later received a big boost because the Hibernia workers saw what CEP was willing to do for the twenty-five people who had lost their jobs. The CEP took up the cause of the fired workers and, instead of taking the conventional route and claiming that they were fired for union activity, made a savvy decision to base the case on a section of the labour law stipulating that workers have a right to reasonably expect certain things from their employers.

In the case of Hibernia, the CEP local argued that the company had done so much indoctrination about its family being there for the life of the project that it seemed reasonable for workers to expect that this would happen, particularly because the company had been so liberal with notes for workers who needed to go to the bank in search of mortgage money. The case dragged on for months, during which time the CEP lawyer also brought up the issue of the statutory freeze on terms and conditions of employment while an application for certification is before the labour board. Termination of a job seemed to be a change in the conditions of employment. After all the legal wrangling, the board ruled in favour of the twenty-five workers and ordered them reinstated – though the decision was later overturned by a Newfoundland Supreme Court decision (the union appealed that decision). Hibernia Management and Development Corporation immediately appealed on a technicality, leaving the workers in limbo. "Callous" was what Ray Cluney called how the company handled the thing from beginning to end.

"These people were hard workers, they had a good reputation," he said. "We offered our services and said 'Look, we're going to take this up on your behalf.'

◀ *Construction of the Hibernia platform, one of the biggest in the world, was completed at Bull Arm, Nfld. in summer 1997.*

If you're going to organize people, you don't just turn your back on them."

In the course of the long journey through the courts and the countless trips to St. John's and all the technical delays cooked up by the company, Daisy changed her mind about unions. She had worked several jobs: quality control on a big dragger on the Grand Banks, janitorial services for the school board, and similar work at Bull Arm, where the big offshore platform was being built. She had been a union member before, but she was surprised by what happened after she was fired.

"I was always leery about unions," she recalled. "But CEP is a different kind of union. They're there for the people. They've proven that over and over for the twenty-five of us who were laid off from Hibernia."

Since that time Daisy and the others have been receiving $200 cheques every week from CEP. Whenever she has to drive from Southern Harbour to St. John's for yet another hearing, CEP pays for travel, hotel, and meal expenses. If she has questions about how the case is dragging on, she only has to contact one of the organizers.

"What really amazes me is that CEP doesn't really even know if they're going to stay on that platform. They're not even collecting dues out there yet and they're still standing by the people. This is definitely a type of union that I've never seen before, and I've worked for a good many unions."

"I was always leery about unions," she recalled. "But CEP is a different kind of union. They're there for the people."

A high-stakes contest

"PEOPLE SAY LAW," wrote Ralph Waldo Emerson, "but they mean wealth."

All the delays are due to the stalling of a company apparently willing to spend whatever it takes on lawyers to prevent Daisy from getting her job back and to stop CEP from representing the workers who voted in a clear majority in its favour. CEP has become familiar with all of this over the ten years of its history because Bell Canada, another multi-billion-dollar company, has dragged workers through the courts in order to avoid meeting its legal obligation to pay women equally. Companies like to use the legal system. They have deep pockets. For the union, it may be part of the game, but it is a frustrating part.

The last thing that oil companies involved in offshore production want is the contagion of unionism spreading south from Newfoundland down the eastern seaboard to the Gulf of Mexico.

They fear that CEP's Hibernia success will give the union a strong lever to organize other platforms. The legal delays are a way of sending a message to workers elsewhere. The message? "Even if the union wins a vote, we will still use our financial power to prevent you from being represented by the union for as long as we can."

For the workers who helped to organize Hibernia, it has been a lesson in the value of a merged union. None of CEP's founding unions would have had the resources to carry on the fight with the oil cartel. The multinationals are willing to spend whatever it takes, perhaps going all the way to the Supreme Court, to stop Daisy Parsons from getting her job back and to stop CEP from representing her. In the meantime, the union is a service organization that is being prevented from providing service, a negotiating organization that can't negotiate. Ron Smith has found it frustrating to deal with companies like this.

"Them being in the courts is like terrorism. Terrorists only have to exist to win. That's all. They only have to show up once in a while, kill a few people, and they win by existing. The companies do that with the courts. They use the courts to win just by existing. Nobody can even remember when they last won a decision. But they keep going back."

CEP intends to keep coming back to the offshore oil industry. It is an article of faith for Atlantic region vice-president Max Michaud: "When we got certified at Hibernia we wrote a page of history. It was the first platform to be organized in North America. And it was very important for us to establish that we're the union in the oil industry."

CHAPTER THREE

J. GORMAN

The bittersweet taste of Purdy's Chocolates

VANCOUVER'S DOWNTOWN ROBSON STREET: tourists from Tokyo, Seattle, and Hamburg stroll along, gazing at the Tommy Hilfiger, The Gap, and Banana Republic displays, trying on the most recent fashion statements jetted in from Mauritius, Honduras, and China. The strip retails all the flash and grab that global business has to offer. Even when the weather is damp and cool, people lounge about in front of the cafés, where Registered Coffee Associates take orders for lattes and mochachinos. The companies concentrate just as hard on studying the demographics of people willing to pay $3.50 for a cup of Jamaican or Kenyan coffee as they do on buying the beans and researching hot new retail locations.

One intersection even has two Starbucks outlets. A few doors along from one of them there's a small storefront with lots of purple trim. It's a new store run by a local chocolate business. Purdy's has decided to take on Toblerone and Ferrero Rocher right on Robson Street. The Purdy's pitch is so corny that it is an appealing contrast to the upmarket outfits.

▲ *"Because we all come from different countries, we have our different cultures, different customs. We share our happiness, we share our sadness." Purdy's workers Kristine Plant, Wendy Stewart, Elsa Aguilar, Helen Chin, Juliet Odejar, Penny Dean with national rep Joie Warnock.*

The Flavelles took over in 1963 and have been running the place ever since, producing "hand-crafted" chocolates from old "traditional family recipes" and packing them in the trademark purple boxes.

"Hi, my name is Philbert and I'm a Hedgehog! I'm a real smooth, sweet guy with every reason to celebrate life! I love my nightly baths in rich and creamy, smooth milk chocolate. I love taking long, romantic walks in Choklit Park ..."

"Choklit Park"? Sure enough, there it is, out on the Kingsway in an old neighbourhood of central Vancouver, right beside a purple fountain cobbled together from old candy-making machines. There, in front of the Purdy's factory, a neatly trimmed hedge surrounds some used tires painted purple and arranged to form a children's play area. Choklit Park.

Back downtown, inside the outlet store, the friendly uniformed women of the Retail Team bustle around amidst glistening displays of chocolate, nuts, and other confections. Shoppers learn about how Purdy's, the largest chocolate retailer in Western Canada, has been a family business ever since it was founded back in 1907. The Flavelles took over in 1963 and have been running the place ever since, producing "hand-crafted" chocolates from old "traditional family recipes" and packing them in the trademark purple boxes. Purdy's sells its products not just down on Robson Street but also at its big Kingsway outlet and at forty-three other stores in British Columbia and Alberta.

The company projects an image of old-fashioned family values and a commitment to quality and small-scale, kitchen conditions. Mr. Purdy's recipes are apparently still being used in the factory, where the Manufacturing Team works. "Every employee is committed to creating a quality product," Purdy's president Karen Flavelle says. "We're fortunate to have such dedicated people working with us." The company proclaims its pride in its "turn of the century production methods" and in being an "employer of choice."

A stroll around the back of the factory, however, reveals a weathered chain-link fence topped by six strands of shiny new barbed wire, a legacy of the strike of 2001. This is where Teresa Yuen, Lynne Wong, and the other women who make the chocolate walked the picket line for over five months. About four out of five of the Purdy's workers are women, and they are hard workers who can put in long hours. "When I started at Purdy's I worked five days a week, eight hours a day, year round," explained Teresa Yuen, adding that there were occasional seasonal layoffs. "They called me part-time."

"Individually crafted" – and collectively challenged

THE CULTURE OF FAMILIES is bound up with stories, and reminiscences. At a gathering of members of CEP Local 2000, raucous laughter greeted the end of each story as several women tried to get a word in edgewise to pass on the latest gossip. It was very noisy. Most of the women were in their forties and

◀ *Strikers at the Purdy's*
Chocolates plant.
Left to Right:
Penny Dean, Jo-Anne
Witham, Lynne Wong,
Maria Amor, and
Margaret Florence.

early fifties, with a fair sprinkling of grandmothers. The bonds were forged by working together, meeting together, walking in front of the barbed wire together. The get-together generated much more of a cozy, family feeling than anything conjured up by Purdy's advertising images. But it was also punctuated by the odd phrase that sounded like it came from a labour board hearing: "reasonable expectation," "our own free will."

In 1996, before the Easter chocolate rush began to peak, the company decided it needed to introduce a ten-hour day to meet the demand. So it put together an ad hoc committee made up of people from each department. Unfortunately for the company, it asked Teresa Yuen to help out. It was the start of a bitter, six-year struggle for the Purdy's workers.

Teresa arrived in Canada from Macau some thirty years ago. By the time she was called on by the company to help them meet their production needs, she was fed up. To her it was obvious that the company was labelling full-time workers part-time to avoid covering the benefits, pensions, and sick leave that went along with full-time status. Working shoulder to shoulder with people doing the same work but knowing that some of them could get their kids' teeth fixed without worrying about the cost, while others couldn't, was bad enough. But worse, because they were not classified as full-timers Teresa and many of the other immigrant women did not qualify for a profit-sharing plan. Every year the company handed the full-timers cheques for as much as $2,000, but the part-timers got nothing.

Penny Dean noticed the corrosive atmosphere as soon as she began working there. She was told to avoid certain people, not to communicate with others. She watched as women fled from the production floor in tears because of how

D. BOUZEK

Purdy's employee ▲
Teresa Yuen arranged
for a dozen or so Asian
and Filipina women
to meet with CEP's
Dave Coles.

front-line supervisors treated them. Penny saw clearly how the system worked in December, when one of the supervisors would let everyone know that her birthday was coming up. If you put in money for a gift, your name got on the card and you found that, come the seasonal layoffs, your chances of being among the last laid off and the first brought back tended to improve.

Physical barriers augmented the other divides. People hired to work in the warehouse space, a room separated from the production area, kept to themselves. Warehouse workers would be classified as full-timers – with all the accompanying benefits – as soon as they were hired. The two groups lived in two different worlds. It was years before Margaret Florence even realized that the workers who made the chocolates that filled the warehouse where she did keyboarding work were being treated differently than she was. "I started to find out about the people who had been there for so many years and were never hired on full-time," she recalled.

It all became too much for Teresa Yuen, who decided to contact the authorities. She hoped that the government would be able to bring a measure of justice to her workplace. Her first move was to get in touch with the B.C. Labour Relations Board, only to learn that Purdy's or any other employer has no obligation to recognize seniority. As long as there was no union they were also free to practise favouritism. In other words, when supervisors make it clear that gifts and payoffs are required to keep your paycheque coming, there's not much you can do about it. This sort of abuse of power was commonplace back at the turn of the century, when it had often been a spur to union organizing drives.

Purdy's workers ▶
are honoured by the
Pacific Northwest Labour
History Association,
June 8, 2002.

Teresa had been making chocolate for six years by that time. The more she thought about it, the madder she got about working full-time but being denied the benefits of full-time classification. "They hand-picked," she said.

Teresa's next move was to write a letter to someone she knew she could trust, Jenny Kwan. A veteran Vancouver city counsellor, Jenny Kwan had gone on to Victoria as the NDP member for the predominantly immigrant provincial riding of Vancouver-Mount Pleasant. But her message was essentially the same as the one delivered by the labour board office. Without a union, Teresa and the others had few workplace rights. The B.C. *Employment Standards Act* provides non-union workers with minimum rights, such as minimum wage, vacation entitlement, and hours of work, but offers no strong means of enforcing those rights. Unionized workers can negotiate far stronger rights in their collective agreements, and they can have a grievance procedure with the possibility of third-party arbitration to enforce the rights.

It wasn't long before Teresa had arranged for a dozen or so Asian and Filipina women to meet with CEP's Dave Coles, who had first learned about trade unions in a Vancouver Island paper mill where the work rules were well established. Coles immediately sensed that the women had already done a lot for themselves. His pitch took longer than usual because it was peppered with technical questions about how seniority works in a union shop and how labour law can protect workers from vindictive management during an organizing drive. Everyone signed a card that evening. Coles was impressed by the workers' determination and know-how.

"They were clearly in charge," the veteran organizer recalled. "They were about to embark on this activity after a fair amount of thought."

In 1997 Teresa and a small core of activists began to go quietly about the business of signing up members. The Purdy's plant was a workplace riddled with distrust, fear, and repressed anger, so they had to tread carefully when approaching someone who had invested heavily in sucking up to the bosses. She felt that the work was "dangerous," but she took comfort in having CEP backing. Whenever she was not sure of something, she called the Vancouver office. "They'd teach me, let me know how to do it."

Soon Teresa had three jobs: one at the chocolate factory, one doing the cooking, cleaning, and laundry at home, and one carefully shopping around to find people who might support the organizing drive. It didn't hurt that when she had first started to work at Purdy's a management flexibility scheme had rotated her through several departments and allowed her to become acquainted with lots of her co-workers. Still, it took a lot of work. And it produced gut-wrenching anxiety.

▲ *"Most of us were organized in industrial workplaces that were mostly white male. Ever since I was hired as an organizer it's been my goal to have our union reflect the communities that we live in."*

• DAVE COLES

In 1997 Teresa and a small core of activists began to go quietly about the business of signing up members. She felt that the work was "dangerous," but she took comfort in having CEP backing.

Workers laid off during the usual December shutdown began to receive courier packages informing them that they had no need of a union because they had such a good employer.

"Every night after dinner, after doing my house job, I started my time in the kitchen picking up the phone. If I didn't trust a person, I passed their name to the CEP. It's really hard. During that period – I think it took almost half a year – I couldn't eat well. I couldn't sleep well. In the middle of the night I always woke up and I couldn't go back to sleep. I was always thinking, 'Will I lose my job? Will the company close down?' It's a big worry. I lost almost ten pounds."

In the end, it paid off. By July 1997 over half of the Purdy's workers had signed CEP cards and the bargaining unit received formal certification. This turned out to be only a first step in dealing with a company that had a noticeably vitriolic attitude towards those members of its Manufacturing Team whom it saw as disloyal. Workers laid off during the usual December shutdown began to receive courier packages informing them that they had no need of a union because they had such a good employer. Returning to work, the newest members of CEP Local 2000 found that Purdy's was attempting to make good on its claim. It addressed their festering resentment about "part-time" workers being excluded from benefits and bonuses by changing their titles. They would now be classified as "prime-time."

This non-solution disgusted the CEP members, but there was more to come before they would get their first contract. As soon as the period prohibiting decertification expired, "certain employees" applied to the labour board to decertify CEP. A new word entered the shop-floor vocabulary: "decert." One of the workers who supported the decert was Margaret Florence, the warehouse worker who later reported on how surprised she had been about certain of the workers being treated differently than others. A male worker asked Margaret to photocopy the decert papers and she agreed. She subsequently devoted many hours of her free time, putting out bulletins to counter union arguments and generally campaigning to get rid of the CEP.

"I basically worked against the union," she said. "And I almost won the decert except for a few votes."

A vote was conducted in June 1998, but the results were sealed because of irregularities. There had been anti-union leafleting inside the plant, and thirty recently hired temporary workers had been allowed to vote. The labour board ordered a second vote, and before that happened the Purdy's workers ratified their first contract. Favouritism took a big hit. Everyone working full-time was classified as such. The company had to lay people off according to seniority and began to move money from its let-us-decide profit-sharing plan into a benefit fund that would include all the workers. When they counted the second decert vote, CEP won by seven ballots.

When she was summoned to company president Karen Flavelle's office after this, Margaret Florence expected a nod of appreciation, thanks for her anti-union efforts. What she got instead were some instructions on what to do next. When she was sent to a lawyer the company had hired on behalf of its backers, with instructions to launch another decert, the lawyer told Margaret that it would not be a good idea. The union was bound to point to employer collusion. So she went about her work as before until management arbitrarily changed her assignment and she heard through the grapevine that her performance was inadequate.

"I said to my supervisor, 'This is a union issue.' I'm not going to tolerate this. I went right to the union and said 'Get me a card!' I've been fighting ever since. It's been a real battle."

Margaret's organizing skills have proved helpful to CEP, and she later became secretary of the bargaining unit. Evidently, Purdy's management is not only harsh. They are also lacking in the smarts necessary to figure out who their friends are.

Creating an environment of unionization

LOCAL 2000 IS A BIG COMPOSITE local with fifty certifications across British Columbia. It represents 2,300 workers in newspapers, commercial printing, and other businesses. Joie Warnock worked in the Pacific Press library before she became a CEP rep handling the Purdy's bargaining unit. Her job description takes her to storefront strike offices in East Vancouver as well as to the streets of Hong Kong, where she found herself in the fall of 2001. Attending a meeting of labour organizers from across the Asia-Pacific region, Joie noticed how many young Asian women there were in the forefront of a movement against corporate globalization.

"If we don't continue to organize, then across the bargaining table the employer will come back at us and say 'The non-union shop across the street is only paying this much.'"

◀ *"That's the reality that CEP has to face head on," Raymond said. "We have to make inroads into the ethnic communities." Viva Pharmaceutical workers with organizer Raymond Louie (3rd from right).*

J. CORMAN

Victory over the ▲
chocolate company is
sweet! Elsa Aguilar wrote
a song about the Purdy's
struggle, and sang it,
accompanied by CEP
national rep David
Durning on his guitar.

For Joie, the anti-globalization movement extends well beyond the images of masked rioters in Seattle or Genoa that prove so attractive to the mainstream media. It is the globalization-as-solidarity percolating everywhere as workers' movements from around the world come together to share information and strategies about campaigns against slave labour in Burma, for worker rights in China, and against sweatshops just about everywhere.

"The Hong Kong meeting was amazing," she said, describing the scene at Temple Street Park in the heart of working-class Kowloon. "Standing there watching the organization of the rally where there were lots of young women in leadership roles was really striking."

Another CEP activist to come out of Vancouver's newspaper industry is Raymond Louie, a rank and file member of Local 2000 seconded to work as an organizer. Raymond, a mail-room worker, got involved in the Purdy's struggle after CEP beat back the first decertification effort. His organizing activities have focused on workplaces that reflect the changing ethnic composition of the Vancouver scene. "That's the reality that CEP has to face head on," Raymond said. "We have to make inroads into the ethnic communities."

His analysis would earn top marks in an industrial relations seminar, though Raymond has learned about unionism on the front lines. He is well aware that the large workplaces like paper mills and oil refineries are all organized. What's more, they are shrinking in size. Employers in small shops where recent immigrants work are notoriously anti-union. Although bad bosses are an organizer's best allies, that doesn't make the job any easier, particularly if you get fired for your efforts. Raymond figured CEP has no choice in the matter.

"If we don't go this route and don't continue to organize, then our union density as a whole is going to go down. That's where our bargaining power comes from. Because across the bargaining table the employer will come back at us and say 'The non-union shop across the street is only paying this much.' Our job is to create an environment of unionization."

In the case of Purdy's, even after the first contract the employer apparently had trouble accepting CEP's right to represent the workers. Raymond believed that the owners view the union as an outsider. Efforts to arrive at a second collective agreement fizzled after the first two-year deal expired in 2000. This gave rise to a bitter five-and-a-half-month strike starting in April 2001. When workers opposed to the union became scabs it added to the anger. Elsa Aguilar, who started at Purdy's at the same time as Teresa Yuen did, grew increasingly frustrated when she watched the trucks coming and going and the scabs laughing in the faces of the strikers. The whole experience was new to her. She is from El Salvador, where labour organizing is a high-stakes game in which both sides play for keeps. Elsa believed that the scabs simply did not understand what it means to someone like her to be free to join a union.

"In my country if you belong to the union, you are persecuted, you are killed," she said. "So it's very scary to belong to a union."

If Canadians took a look around the world they would realize how fortunate they are to have the right to organize without risking their lives. She was particularly disgusted by the scabs who claimed that the reason CEP got involved was to take money from them. Indeed, the Purdy's affair probably cost CEP far more than it would ever recoup in membership dues.

But labour organizing is not about narrow cost-benefit considerations. Dave Coles, who started organizing in 1981 and went on to become Western vice-president, said he has never been asked the question "Will you ever get your money back?" when it comes to an organizing drive. "We go out and organize workers who need to be organized," he said. "If you get that reputation, you'll get the easy ones along with the hard ones. It's my experience that opportunities come to you when you fight the big fight. That's because you're out in public, standing up for workers."

The Purdy's strike became something of a cause célèbre in the B.C. labour movement, pitting as it did a group of immigrant workers, mostly women, against a company that maintained a high retail profile. Although some voices called for an organized boycott of Purdy's chocolate, CEP did nothing to deliberately tarnish the company's folksy, down-home image. That would have jeopardized jobs. Still, a high-profile strike against a company producing a luxury product in a heavily unionized province probably had its effect, particularly on Purdy's group purchase plans in organized workplaces. The company cemented its anti-union reputation when, after the strike entered its sixth month, a labour board ruling decertified the union on a technicality. There was an allegation that, back in 1997, there had been irregularities with the cards signed during the original organizing campaign. The strike ended, and the workers had to decide once again whether they wanted to sign CEP cards. The labour board supervised a new certification vote immediately after the strike ended, but the company objected to that and used the resulting legal delays to hire twenty-one "temporary" employees. It argued that they should be allowed to participate in any new certification ballot, though CEP disagreed.

All of this put union workers at a disadvantage. The CEP was legally forced to the sidelines for three and a half months while it waited for the labour board to decide on its recertification application. The company was free to get its message out in the plant during this period, although CEP continued to rent the former strike headquarters across the road. The storefront on the Kingsway was a use-

> "In my country if you belong to the union, you are persecuted, you are killed," Elsa Aguilar said. "So it's very scary to belong to a union."

> "I like my co-workers,
> they are fantastic.
> We're always
> talking about
> children
> and husbands and
> family stuff."
> • TERESA YUEN

ful meeting place and organizing headquarters. The company hoped the newly hired workers would tip the balance in its favour should the board order another ballot. The union was confident enough that it dropped its objections to allowing the newly hired workers to vote. On January 31, 2002, the union won by five votes. Purdy's rewarded the newly hired workers by terminating their jobs, thus confirming their "temporary" status.

Lynne Wong could not understand why the chocolate company was so stubbornly opposed to its workers' right to organize. A twelve-year employee who only became full-time after eight years in the production area, she acted as a spokesperson for Chinese-speaking workers, who believed that because she had attended school in Canada her English was better than theirs. This, of course, got her into a lot of trouble with management. But after the final certification vote she remained more puzzled than angry. She could not figure out why Purdy's would risk losing both production and its carefully cultivated reputation rather than dealing with its workers in a straightforward way – why it would spend so much management time and money on fighting with its workers instead of tending to the business of its business. "They have a good company," she said. "I really wish they would sit down, bargain, and accept the fact that we are organized."

After the strike ended the video cameras inside the plant remained. So did the tension. But, for the union supporters at least, that stress was balanced off by a new sense of solidarity. Teresa Yuen believed that the women had

After a roller-coaster ► *ride of wins and setbacks, the union at Purdy's won recertification by five votes.*

been brought closer together by their days on the picket line and all the other adversities they had faced.

"The company is still trying to break us," she said. "The more they keep trying, the more we are strong. I like my co-workers, they are fantastic. We are always talking about family things. Because we all came from different countries, we have our different cultures, different customs. We're always talking about children and husbands and family stuff. We share our happiness, we share our sadness."

By April 2002, exactly a year after they went on strike for a better contract, the Purdy's workers had something else to be glad about. They ratified their second contract, an agreement that gave them ninety-two cents an hour over three years as well as improvements in vacation pay and bereavement leave. New job categories and more stewards boosted union strength. Most important, however, was the recognition by the company of the employees' right to belong to a union. The issue of a union shop and dues checkoff for all employees was referred to arbitration. Within a few months an arbitrator found in favour of Local 2000, accepting the union proposal for new union security language in the collective agreement. All employees were to become union members as a condition of employment.

From a candy factory to a "Media Union"

WHEN SHE WENT TO HER FIRST executive meeting of CEP Local 2000, Penny Dean began wondering what she had gotten herself into. It was a world apart from her experience in the bakers and confectioners union. It was like something out of some obscure service club where they had secret handshakes and such like. There was talk of chapel rooms, lobster shifts, dark shifts. She and the vice-president of the Purdy's unit were so intimidated at first that when someone called a vote, they didn't raise their hands. They figured it was not fair to vote on something they did not understand. The chair of the meeting asked them why they hadn't voted.

"Then we felt guilty because we didn't vote," she said, recalling how green she was in 1997.

Starting something new and different can be intimidating, like moving to a new city and starting at a new school as a kid. It makes all the difference if the people at the new place welcome you and take the trouble to make you feel like you belong. She worked in a candy factory and here she was in the middle of a huge outfit calling itself "the Media Union." Five years after her first meeting of Local 2000, she was feeling more at home. Indeed, she had become chair of the Purdy's unit of the local.

J. GORMAN

▲ *Penny Dean became chair of the Purdy's unit of Local 2000. "We've definitely been shown what CEP stands for.... They don't differentiate. If only our company treated us like our union does."*

"We've definitely been shown what the CEP stands for," she explained. "Whether you're a Pacific Press person making twenty-five or thirty dollars an hour or us at Purdy's, they support you the same. They don't differentiate. If only our company treated us like our union does."

The Purdy's workers are by and large in their forties and fifties. They like working regular days with weekends off, in some cases to spend time with their young grandchildren. Amy McDonal is younger than most of her fellow chocolate workers. Like other workers in the warehouse, she was hired on with full benefits right away. She had trouble figuring out what was going on with the union so she voted against certification at first. Now, after what she calls "the fight," she feels as though she is always being watched. But the feelings she has developed for her fellow workers balance it off.

"I'm more friends with the people now than I ever was when I started there," she said. "I don't know much about unions. This is the first one I've ever been involved in. The CEP has put out so much for us. Paying our strike pay. We'd only been unionized for a few years. The amount of money we put in and the amount of money they put out, they really have put themselves out to make us feel like we're important. We're quite a small bargaining unit but they've made us feel like we're a group of a thousand, not a hundred."

For Dave Coles, the struggle at Purdy's was all about a union rooted in today's communities. "It's our responsibility to reflect society. Most of us were organized in industrial workplaces that were mostly white male. Ever since I was hired as an organizer it's been my goal to have our union reflect the communities that we live in. In central Vancouver, the Purdy's operation reflects the community."

CHAPTER FOUR

CP PHOTO

"...To the very end" –
PAY EQUITY AND JOB LOSS AT BELL

JUST UP FROM the busy downtown intersection of Princess and Division streets in Kingston, Ont., there's a two-storey limestone building that looks as solid as Old Fort Henry, the city's main tourist attraction. Above the main door is an old-fashioned corporate coat of arms: a chunky metal bell surrounded by the words "The Bell Telephone Company of Canada, Local and Long Distance Telephone." That was the old phone company, which was once a busy place that housed a crowd of operators. Today, right across the street is a modern concrete office building sporting the company's new, designer logo.

On the cold, blustery January day I went there, the sixty or so women milling around in front of the place were not paying much attention to old logos designed to project an image of reliability. They knew better. It was a noisy crowd. "We want the company to know we won't go away quietly!"

Donna Peterson shouted something about pay equity into a bullhorn that

▲ *Operators and technicians denounce Bell's plan to sell jobs to a U.S. company. Montreal, January 1999.*

had been painted light green and decorated with a CEP sticker.

"Pay us what we're worth!" hollered Barb Davidson, another woman who was clearly not going to go away quietly.

Many of the Kingston operators are women in their forties. Like Peterson, they have nearly twenty-five years' seniority and get $19.50 an hour. Donna Peterson said she was worried that the new, contracted-out jobs would be down in the ten-dollar range. But other work was not easy to come by.

"Where are we going to go to start over?" Donna asked. The strike of 1999 had been precipitated by Bell's announcement that it was selling off local jobs to a U.S. company.

"If you came to Bell from high school – and most of us did – you haven't worked for anyone else. You don't have other expertise. You're stuck in that little niche. Most of us had the impression we were going to be there until we retired."

According to business-page logic, these comments seem old-fashioned, almost quaint. Employers love to go on about no job being secure anymore. They drum the message home through the media and at the bargaining table. The corporate media (BCE – Bell Canada Enterprises – also owns *The Globe and Mail* and CTV) repeat it too. The f-word of the labour market. "Learn to be flexible. Expect to have a dozen different jobs in your life."

Their employer told the women at Kingston's telephone office to be flexible. They would be offered jobs with the new phone centre company. It didn't happen. Instead, the promised jobs never materialized in Kingston. Of course,

> Employers love to go on about no job being secure anymore. They drum the message home through the media and at the bargaining table. The corporate media . . . repeat it too. The f-word of the labour market. "Learn to be flexible. Expect to have a dozen different jobs in your life."

Ma Bell's children ▶ *say: "Enough is enough."* *May 1999.*

P. KEIGHLEY

the women at Bell were used to broken promises. Bell kept forcing CEP into court with a series of legal tactics that allowed it to stall on its commitment to meet its pay equity obligations. In 2001 BCE reported a profit of half a billion dollars.

Many of the operators that Bell tossed out in Quebec and Ontario had been with Bell since high school. When she started, said Odette Gagnon of Montreal, "It was a pretty paternalistic company. 'Everything's a family,' and all that." Bell was once very visible in the local community, arranging for operators to visit schools, explaining to the kids never to answer the phone and tell someone that there was nobody home. They would explain 911. At Christmas time they used to visit senior citizens homes and make long distance calls for them. Things have changed.

The Kingston operators had placed a summertime lawn chair on the snowy sidewalk. Seated there was a life-sized granny doll, the very image of "Ma Bell." The rosy-cheeked lady had a phone cradled on her shoulder and she was holding a CEP picket sign that said "Hello? Bell? You treat your workers very badly." The Limestone City Raging Grannies were there to sing songs in support of the CEP members. One of them was also holding a sign. It said "Grannies Against Greed."

The great pay equity case

ODETTE GAGNON no longer works for Bell. Like two thousand other operators in Quebec and Ontario she was given the choice of taking alternative work with Nordia or accepting a layoff package. But as a long-time unionist, she was keeping busy at the union hall upstairs from a printing company in Montreal, fielding calls from women all over Quebec. Some had retired. Some had taken the voluntary severance package. A handful were among the survivors, still working at the few operator jobs that still exist in the Bell system. They were all curious about what was happening with The Case.

Not many people could attend the Canadian Human Rights Tribunal hearings in Ottawa, so the women counted on Odette and other CEP activists to keep in touch. Sometimes, when the courts were about to come down with yet another decision in response to yet another of Bell's legal challenges, Odette would charter a bus to go to Ottawa. There was a spirit of quiet determination on Highway 417, coupled with a feeling that it was good to be together again.

"Operators are always there," Odette said. "They are well-informed. They follow the case's progress and the union keeps us up to date."

... continued on page 54

▲ *Not many operators could attend the Human Rights hearings in Ottawa, so they counted on Odette and other activists to keep in touch. Odette Gagnon addresses a rally, May 5, 1999.*

Privatized phone company learns a lesson

THERE WAS A TIME when the Manitoba Telephone System had the job of providing efficient, affordable phone service to all the province's citizens. Then, after the usual promises of People's Capitalism, it became Manitoba Telecom Services.

The new company, promised the politicians who supported privatization, would be so strong that it would not need rate increases any time soon. Shares would be offered on the open market, and Manitobans would have the chance to own their own phone company. The magic of the market would, once again, prove so much better than the heavy hand of the state.

As CEP predicted, it didn't turn out that way. The new MTS immediately began to raise rates, along with executive salaries. It was not long before the president was getting an $83,000 raise to go along with his $93,000 bonus. As for owning the phone company, all Manitobans had already owned the firm, which had been operating in their interests. Now it operated in the interests of a group of shareholders, many of whom were outside the province.

"A company we all owned was sold to a small group of Manitobans who had enough spare cash to play the market," said Winnipeg journalist Doug Smith as the extent of the swindle became obvious. "It was sold to them at a bargain basement price. The government even loaned them the money to buy the stock. They started to sell their shares as soon as the price began to rise. It was bound to, since the government had set the selling price so low."

The end of this familiar story had been predicted by CEP and all the others who had backed the Save MTS! campaign. CEP locals 7 and 55, representing clerical and operator staff at the phone company, knew that a privatized company would not only mean trouble for telephone subscribers but also cause headaches at the bargaining table. As it turned out, that prediction was also well founded.

In early 1999 the phone workers were confronted with an "or else" attitude and a threatening tone. The new regime at MTS was determined to gut the job-security provisions of the contract by eliminating the language stipulating that the employer could not contract out any work while any member was on layoff. To underline their determination, the new MTS bosses – a whole new cadre of union-busters had been brought in after privatization – locked out the men in the craft services, represented by a different union.

That dispute was settled in a few days, but the

The membership gave their bargaining committee an 88.5 per cent strike mandate. But the bargaining committee also made a shrewd decision. Instead of going on strike, the union would provoke the company to lock them out.

▲ *Locked-out MTS workers line up at the paper shredder to let the company know what they think of the privatized company's latest offer.*

company figured that it had accomplished its goal, which was to throw a scare into the CEP women.

That strategy didn't work. Indeed, it backfired. The membership gave their bargaining committee an 88.5 per cent strike mandate. But the bargaining committee also made a shrewd decision. Instead of going on strike, the union would provoke the company to lock them out. That way the workers would gain maximum sympathy from a public still resentful about the privatization of the phone company.

"As CEP we were not strangers to the public because of the campaign to save MTS," explained CEP's Maggi Hadfield. "Here they were locking out the most vulnerable employees, the women."

Setting the trap that would sucker management into locking the doors was a tricky business that required careful co-ordination and maximum secrecy. On June 2 the members across Manitoba all unplugged from their computers at the same time. They proceeded to study the manuals, visit the water fountain, head for the washroom, check a few files, and discuss the weather. All of this caused a frantic scramble among managers, many of whom didn't know how to handle incoming calls. Ten minutes later, after a signal from the chief stewards, regular service was suddenly restored. The head office told the local managers to stay all night, just in case.

That was alright, because there was no action planned until the next day, when chaos hit MTS again, this time for half an hour. The women at a dozen locations in Winnipeg and just as many outside the capital suddenly stopped work. At three o'clock that afternoon the phone rang at CEP headquarters.

"'This is crazy!' barked the head of Industrial Relations. "We can't run a business like this. We're locking your members out."

"Oh, no . . ." said Maggi, as she smiled at the other women in the room. "That's terrible."

The fifteen hundred members of locals 7 and 55 spent exactly a hundred days on the picket line. Whether it was a strike or a lockout didn't matter so much as that it turned into a fine summer of picketing, picnics, and parades.

"A lot of the women showed up for four hours on the line and spent the rest of the day with their kids," said Diane Shaver, who worked as a picket captain. "For an awful lot of them it was the best summer they had ever had."

The MTS managers were cooped up inside trying to keep the system working, calling the newspaper to take out ads that talked about the "CEP strike." Meanwhile, pickets in Morden held Mexican Days, Hawaiian Days, and Western ▶

▲ *Maggi Hadfield, Fred Pomeroy, and Ron Carlson discuss bargaining strategy to counter MTS proposals to gut job security provisions.*

Days, with festive clothing to match. There was Hair Dyeing Day in Thompson. The annual parade at the Selkirk Fair featured a CEP float. There were pancake breakfasts, pizza days, and BBQs.

All the while the members kept contributing recipes to the cookbook that they had started to compile before the lockout began. It was a fundraiser for the Spina Bifida and Hydrocephalus Association, CEP's charity of choice. When the one-hundred-page book came out it had a postscript describing how the union people saw a labour dispute in which a member had her bridal shower on the picket line: "We never lost sight of the positive aspect – more family time." After being asked how things were going on the picket line, one eight-year-old girl

It was all familiar to any trade unionist who had ever organized a strike or walked a picket line, but there was one difference. It was organized by and for women, and that gave it a flavour all its own.

answered, "MTS was mean and locked my mom out, but we fooled them. We're having fun."

It was not all fun and games, though. The activists who organized all the actions were run ragged. No one could have known that the employer would eventually capitulate just after Labour Day. It takes organizing savvy to know when a group shows signs of picket fatigue and to respond by making sure the roving social committee arrives right away with some songs, a picnic, and other morale boosters. People attending the MTS Golf Classic got the message that the company was not the good corporate citizen it claimed to be. The Pan Am Games torch run passed through a line of flag-waving CEP members whose banner said: "MTS: Proud Sponsor of 1500 Locked-Out Employees." At many an event the women carried a proud banner of their own, with a reminder of the key role of the phone company women during the Winnipeg General Strike: "TELEPHONE OPERATORS FIRST OUT 7 am May 15 1919."

It was all familiar to any trade unionist who had ever organized a strike or walked a picket line, but there was one difference. It was organized by and for women, and that gave it a flavour all its own. A group in Morden used their time on the picket line to knit an afghan, which they donated to the local women's shelter. Pickets organized a clothing swap for children returning to school.

Then there was the famous sprinkler incident, something that might have been handled differently by male strikers. That one unfolded in East St. Paul when one of CEP's travelling Garden Parties descended on the home of a scab manager to do some secondary picketing. It was the second such party and, instead of welcoming the women, the scab showed his hospitality by turning his sprinkler system on them and calling the police. Instead of confronting the fellow and hurling abuse his way, the pickets simply moved their cars onto that side of the road and began to wash them. By the time the police did arrive, the scab manager was even more livid. The women were having a good time, and the cops were amused.

"You don't need us here to help with all these beautiful ladies," the police told the scab, issuing him a summons for unauthorized spraying of a public area.

Aside from organizing picket lines and lively protests, CEP activists also kept close track of Manitoba premier Gary Filmon, the man who had rammed through the MTS privatization scheme in the face of widespread public opposition. Whenever Filmon and the characters organizing his 1999 election tour got off their bus, there was CEP's white van, all decked out in pompoms. In a scene that was often played out on suppertime newscasts, the premier made his speech with CEP picket signs bobbing up and down in the background. They borrowed their chant from the supporters of Chile's socialist president Salvador Allende: "The people, united, will never be defeated."

The notion of defeat was something that Filmon soon had to get used to. The voters swept his thoroughly discredited government from office, installing an NDP government a few days after the CEP victory at MTS. The telephone workers gained a pay increase, a signing bonus, sick leave for casual part-timers, and a new voluntary termination package. There was no change to the strong contracting-out language that the company had wanted to dilute. Returning to work, the women all wore T-shirts bearing the CEP logo and a simple, three-word message: "Union and proud."

A few weeks later Maggi Hadfield was making small talk with the head of Industrial Relations for MTS, trying to defuse the tensions that had built up over the previous few months. He said he had seen a side of the workers that he had not been aware of.

"You know what your problem is?" she replied. "You took on the men but then you made us mad. And when you tick a woman off, honey, you're going to pay. You're married. You should know that." △

Aside from organizing picket lines and lively protests, CEP activists also kept close track of Manitoba premier Gary Filmon, the man who had rammed through the MTS privatization scheme in the face of widespread public opposition.

The Case started around the time that CEP was formed. It began as a voluntary, co-operative approach, with the company and the union both agreeing to a joint study that would determine once and for all whether female-dominated jobs at the company were paid lower than male-dominated jobs of equal value. Both parties duly conducted the study, and when it was completed the women who worked at Bell had their long-standing suspicions confirmed. There was a big pay equity wage gap.

What had started amicably had become a difficult, expensive legal battle once Bell realized just how much money the *crème de la crème* of wage studies would cost them. When CEP began to try to negotiate, Bell backed off, forcing the union to take the case to the Canadian Human Rights Commission. CEP convinced the commission that it had a strong enough case to warrant an inquiry by the Canadian Human Rights Tribunal.

Since then the tribunal has examined the case on a stop-and-go basis, its proceedings delayed by Bell's preliminary arguments and technical challenges, some of which ended up in federal court. Bell won a few rounds at the lower level, only to lose to CEP on appeal. This did not deter the company from trying again and again to derail The Case, the largest private-sector pay equity case ever in Canada. On one occasion Bell took it to the Supreme Court of Canada, only to be denied again. By the time CEP held its convention in 2002, marking its tenth year as a merged union, it was waiting for another appearance at the Supreme Court. This time Bell was claiming that the

Bell used legal tactics to ▶ stall on its commitment to meet its pay equity obligations. In 2001 BCE reported a profit of half a billion dollars while its workers kept on looking for some respect.

R. HATFIELD

◀ *"In this case alone," says CEP's lawyer, "I have been to federal court on more occasions than in all other cases combined." Bell workers rally one more time in front of the Supreme Court of Canada, April 2001.*

Human Rights Tribunal was not sufficiently impartial for the company to get a fair hearing.

The CEP's lawyer had never been involved in a case with so many objections, so many attempts to delay, so many attempts to dismiss. For Peter Engelmann it was the most extraordinary case he had experienced in twenty years of practice. "An old adage among lawyers is that there is usually an inverse relationship between the number of preliminary technical objections and the merits of one's case," he said. "In this case alone, I've been to federal court on more occasions than I have in any other case. In fact, in all other cases combined."

It would be tempting to argue, as some have done, that Bell was suddenly transformed from a kindly, paternalistic employer into a greedy multinational obsessed with competitiveness and the bottom line. That it had something to do with deregulation of the telephone market. In fact, the old Bell may have been paternalistic, but it was not kindly. The women who worked for Canada's biggest phone company in the old days of monopoly were not allowed to turn their heads while sitting in their work positions. They were obliged to hold up a special card if they wanted to go to the bathroom. Women in small towns were paid differently than women in cities, and nowhere were they paid very well. When the women became sick of being treated like children by a company that thought it had the right to tell them what to do and when to do it, they formed a union.

"They may well have been paternalistic, but work conditions were quite poor," Odette Gagnon said. "We were paid according to our regions. When we became unionized we greatly improved our work conditions, we obtained better salaries and so on."

The women believed that the reason some of them were having trouble getting jobs in the Bell business office across the street was simple enough. "We have CEP stamped on our foreheads," said Donna.

Of course, it was only because the union was there that Bell agreed in the first place to participate in the joint study that revealed the inequality between male and female wages. And for ten years CEP stood up to the company when it tried to avoid its obligations. Bell was so arrogant that one of its legal arguments, if successful, would have resulted in rewriting Canada's pay equity laws. CEP's victories in the fight with Bell have been victories for non-unionized women and women represented by smaller unions confronted by employers who are just as greedy as Bell... if that's possible.

A tough fight . . . and a stubborn determination

THE COMPANY THAT BELL PROMISED would provide jobs for the Kingston operators was called Nordia. Some five hundred jobs were destined for Kingston. The economic development officer at the Chamber of Commerce boasted about the city's competitive advantages. Some women got themselves transferred from other Bell offices slated to close, just so they could get jobs at Nordia. When it became known that this was merely another broken promise, the Bell women began to refer to Nordia wryly as "Nordya." As in, "Nor d'ya have a job, nor d'ya have a pension."

One of them was Barb Davidson, who described herself as a "Bell brat." That's because her father was a Bell supervisor, her godfather was a vice-president, and four of her brothers and sisters went to work for Bell. She started at Bell when she was seventeen and stayed until she was let go twenty years later. She was raised to be anti-union.

The Bell fight wasn't ▼
just for CEP members.
It was a fight for the
rights of all workers.
Recognizing this, the
NDP and CLC leadership
walked the union walk
in support of Bell strikers
in May 1999.

P. KEIGHLEY

R. HATFIELD

▲ *"CEP is ten years old and, unfortunately, so is the Bell pay equity struggle." Quebec vice-president Michel Ouimet addresses a Bell demonstration in Montreal, August, 2002.*

Sitting in the union office under a CEP poster from the *Calgary Herald* strike ("Journalism under Attack"), Barb and Janice Samms and Donna Peterson keep returning to the sense of betrayal that the CEP members in Kingston felt when Bell 1) unilaterally ended their jobs, 2) failed to keep its promise to bring the new subsidiary to town, and 3) refused to employ them in its business office just across Princess Street from the building where they had worked for so many years. Donna was told she did not have the right communications skills.

Barb, clearly an articulate woman, was told that she lacked sales potential. "What a loser I was to come in during the ice storm. What a loser I was not to take all those sick days. What a loser I was to be such a good ambassador for Bell."

Barb had become bitter. After she lost her job she became depressed and began sleeping eighteen hours at a time. She went to counselling, where she learned that she had trouble dealing with loss. While she tended to agree with that assessment, she also had trouble with the company that had always tried hard to cultivate just the right image. "How come you're fucking me over? Because I've done everything you asked, when you asked."

Barb finally did find a low-wage job in a bingo parlour. Her starting pay was fifty cents an hour more than one of the women who was already working there when she was hired, which deeply offended the union sensibilities she picked up in her years as a CEP member: "It's just so wrong ..."

The women believed that the reason some of them were having trouble getting jobs in the Bell business office across the street was simple enough. "We have CEP stamped on our foreheads," said Donna. She was now spending her weeks in Ottawa, where a few jobs in operator services remained in 2002. She did not like leaving her young daughter in Kingston, but had no choice.

Janice, a former steward and vice-president of the CEP local, had found a job working at the front desk at the only unionized hotel in town, starting at $8 an hour, down from $20 at Bell. She figured she was one of the lucky ones. Others were hired at the new call centre. Barb was still looking for something better than a few hours a week at the bingo hall. She figured that she had been an A-plus employee. All the women were proud of their years at Bell. They were good at what they did.

Barb's long months of sending resumés and making follow-up calls and sometimes getting interviews had taught her something. Employers are no longer looking for years of solid experience with one company. Indeed, that is a mark of someone who is "stale" rather than being "flexible." But employers are still wary of women who might be inclined to have children; one advised

The union jobs in Bell's operator services were ideal for working women with young families. There were lots of possibilities of different hours. Once the union came in, the operators suddenly found themselves holding the kinds of stable jobs that men in paper mills and oil refineries had.

Barb to change her resumé to indicate she was "finished with her family." Donna stubbornly refused to hide her work with CEP on her resumé. "It shows I have organizational skills."

The union jobs in Bell's operator services were ideal for working women with young families. There were lots of possibilities of different hours. Once the union came in, the operators suddenly found themselves holding the kinds of stable jobs that men in paper mills and oil refineries had. With that kind of wage and benefit package, a woman could raise a family and send her kids to college, even if she did not have a partner.

Operator services disappeared, replaced by technology that allowed the employer to substitute voice-mail hell for the personal touch and skills of women like Donna and Janice and Barb. Bell shuffled the remaining work off to low-wage subcontractors. Yet the Kingston group kept in touch. They had always been a tight, militant local. Although they no longer shared a workplace, they still shared something that kept them focused, a stubborn determination to see justice done.

"For me it's so based on pay equity . . ." said Barb.

"I'm getting so pissed off about pay equity," interrupted Janice. "It's dragged on so long. We've been fighting it since 1993."

At the beginning, many of the women in the local didn't know much about The Case, Janice explained. But in the mid-1990s it began to sink in. "Oh yeah! The company owes us money . . ." The awareness was heightened when Bell came up with a cash offer that the women across Quebec and Ontario turned down.

From where she sat in Montreal, Odette Gagnon figured that the multibillion-dollar company had been underpaying women for decades. But as long as Bell persisted with the legal technicalities and all the other delaying tactics, it was just prolonging the injustice. "This money was owed to us. This money is owed to women," she said. "They know it. They have known for ten years that there have been unfair practices within Bell, and for us, this is our money. This has gone on for years. The study was done in 1992, but this means that there were salary discrepancies well beforehand."

For CEP, the Bell pay equity fight was about more than social justice and human rights. It had been more than another long struggle by a union that had over the course of its first ten years forged a reputation of taking on the tough fights and seeing them through to the end. It had been about more than the loss of two thousand dues-paying members.

After the founding convention in 1992, the CEP members at Bell operator services made up the single largest group of women in an organization that had just brought together people from male-dominated workplaces – pulp and paper mills, chemical plants, oil refineries. Even the rest of the telephone workers were men. Even with the addition of a media sector with a higher proportion of women than existed in the mills and refineries, CEP remained a union with a small percentage of female members. The loss of the Bell women meant that a male union had suddenly become that much more male. This fact of life would prove to be a significant organizing and organizational challenge.

On the organizing front, the union responded by signing up new members among school support staff in Alberta and clerical workers at the New Brunswick telephone company. On the organizational front, the union put in place a national women's committee. CEP also brought a human rights policy into its constitution. The policy would be a model for the rest of the labour movement.

When those kinds of changes were proposed, the result was some difficult, trying struggles. More than one activist who participated used the word "brutal" to describe them. But in the end CEP kept pushing forward, in the same way it did when it took on Conrad Black at the *Calgary Herald*, or Mobil Oil at Hibernia, or behemoths like Fletcher-Challenge and Abitibi-Consolidated in the forest sector and small companies like Purdy's Chocolates in Vancouver. Along the way, CEP carved out a reputation as a union committed to standing by the principles of the labour movement and seeing struggles through to the end.

Sometimes the conflicts involved bread and butter issues at the bargaining table. Sometimes they meant standing up for workers who were not even union members. Sometimes they involved defending the social programs that protect every citizen. Always they led to one conclusion for anyone watching: this was a union to be reckoned with.

> Sometimes the conflicts involved bread and butter issues at the bargaining table. Sometimes they meant standing up for workers who were not even union members. Sometimes they involved defending the social programs that protect every citizen. Always they led to one conclusion for anyone watching: this was a union to be reckoned with.

◀ *"If the CEP as a union doesn't stand up and fight a case like this, then smaller unions and non-unionized women do not have a chance."*
• CAROL WALL

In spring 2002 CEP human rights director Carol Wall was at a meeting with Bell Canada. They were discussing The Case. Someone on the other side of the table said something. "It made my blood just boil," Carol said later. Carol comes from a working-class family that has union values as part of its genetic code. Her father was a sleeping-car porter and a teamster. The Walls trace their roots to Maryland and two brothers who escaped slavery and came to Canada via the Underground Railroad. She learned as a child that you never, ever, cross a picket line. What she heard from Bell was that the CEP women had expectations that were simply too high, that they just had to lower them.

"If the CEP as a union doesn't stand up and fight a case like this, then smaller unions and non-unionized women do not have a chance," Carol said. "It's important that CEP sees this through to the very end."

CHAPTER FIVE

The Abitibi strike

"BLOWBACK" IS A TERM that became familiar after terrorists knocked down the World Trade Center. It turned out that these were the same people whom the United States had funded and armed to fight the Soviet Union in Afghanistan. A less graphic name for blowback is "unintended consequences."

The world's biggest newsprint company got hit by blowback in 1998.

It happened when Abitibi-Consolidated hatched a plan to weaken the CEP locals at its mills by destroying the long-established practice of pattern bargaining. Negotiating together gave the union more clout at the table and then allowed it to set a pattern that it could use with the other companies in the Eastern pulp and paper industry. Rather than capitulate to a company scheme that would have eroded their bargaining strength, the workers voted to walk off the job. The company assumed that they would do this, and planned to wait them out. Its warehouses were bulging with newsprint and the inventories could see it through a long strike.

Not only that, the company had an additional strategic ploy ready in Ontario, where it had four mills and the employer-friendly Harris government had recently brought in changes to the labour law that mirrored the company's

▲ *The world's biggest newsprint company got hit by blowback in 1998. Pickets at the Abitibi mill, Grand Falls, Nfld.*

"You can negotiate long and hard for many years to establish terms and conditions in a collective agreement. Then with the stroke of a pen a government can take many of those things away from you."
• CEC MAKOWSKI

divide-and-conquer bargaining demands. The Harris Conservatives felt the same way as Abitibi did about weakening unions by splitting them up. So, amidst much talk of "flexibility" (that f-word much favoured by the employing class), the Tories passed a law making it harder to organize new unions and easier to decertify existing ones. It also required that unions representing people at various workplaces of a single company could no longer consolidate strike votes and take collective action across bargaining units.

CEP members at eleven Abitibi mills went on strike June 15, 1998. The company immediately brought in the lawyers and challenged the legality of the Ontario strike vote at the provincial labour relations board. After several days of hearings the board ruled that the strike vote violated the new labour law and ordered CEP locals across the province to conduct a series of independent votes, count them separately, and report the results.

That happened on a Friday. After a weekend of frantic phone calls, plane trips, and hurried meetings, the CEP's Ontario locals had all voted again. Much to Abitibi's disappointment, the strike mandate was even higher, in some cases approaching unanimity. Blowback had begun. Instead of weakening the strike, the company move had given it added momentum.

For Cecil Makowski, CEP Ontario vice-president, Abitibi's support by a right-wing government underlined the importance of union activity in the political arena. That's the reason that CEP invests time and resources in electing labour-friendly governments. "You can negotiate long and hard for many years to establish terms and conditions in a collective agreement. Then with the stroke of a pen a government can take many of those things away from you."

Facing down an employer

DURING THE ABITIBI STRIKE of 1998 the CEP members accomplished three things. First, they said a loud "No" to the company demand that they bargain separately. Philippe Hanna of Local 1455 in Shawinigan summed up that move. "They wanted to negotiate plant by plant, but a plant has no mandate. They can't negotiate. All the orders come from Montreal and Montreal makes all the decisions."

Philippe, a twenty-six-year veteran union activist and president of Local 1455, explained that, if anything, Abitibi was becoming even more centralized in its management style. Local issues that at one time could have been settled locally at the Belgo mill – one of the oldest paper mills in Canada – now had to be referred to the executive suite. The top management was claiming that making a change in one of its mills could have an effect on all of them. For

K. NEWMAN

◀ *"They wanted to negotiate plant by plant, but a plant has no mandate. They can't negotiate. All the orders come from Montreal." Philippe Hanna, Local 1455, Shawinigan.*

Philippe, Abitibi's demand that the big contract issues be negotiated on a mill-by-mill basis was "bizarre."

Second, the strike offered CEP the chance to show how a union that had merged six years before could take on offensive companies. Frank Tremblett of Grand Falls, Nfld., recalled what had happened just after the Canadian Paperworkers Union broke away from the U.S. union in 1975. At that time the companies were saying, "This is a good time to take them on. They're just babies, they've got no money."

"So they took us on," Frank said, "and we began striking all over Canada."

It was a formative strike for the union. Although strike pay was abysmal, the walkout lasted over six months in some locations. Meanwhile, the big paper companies hid behind Ottawa's "Anti-Inflation Board," claiming that they could not meet the union's monetary demands. Frank's local was forced to borrow $1.6 million from the bank in Grand Falls, and that only allowed strike pay of $16 per week plus $5 per child – this for the privilege of spending months freezing on a wintertime picket line.

In Grand Falls, Frank said, "A lot of people got hurt, a lot of people were hungry, and it took a long time to get over it." But, he added, "We had no choice, because if we hadn't done it the companies would have broken us. What it did was it brought us together."

Something similar happened with CEP in 1998, only the hardship wasn't a factor because of the new union's financial muscle and the determined solidarity of its members. The CEP strike pay, already $200 per week, was topped up dramatically in 1998 when locals in the Eastern pulp and paper

... continued on page 67

In Grand Falls, Frank said, "A lot of people got hurt, a lot of people were hungry, and it took a long time to get over it." But, he added, "We had no choice ..."

The occupation of a mill: "We made a difference"

BOB STOREY WAS WEARING his "insiders'" jacket. The group even had its own website: cepinsiders@yahoo.com. He had spent nearly a month sleeping on a narrow cot inside the old paper mill where he had worked for twenty-five years. He had a quick answer to a question about why he was going to so much trouble to support what seemed like a lost cause.

"Maybe it won't help us," he replied, "but it might help someone else."

Bob was one of the twenty CEP members who occupied the Gallaher paper mill in Ontario's Niagara Peninsula for twenty-six days starting in October 1999. The workers had taken over the plant to save their jobs. The mill had opened early in the century and had been a fixture in the small town of Thorold for generations. It still employed some 350 people when it closed in spring 1999.

A year later the mill had not reopened. The occupation was over. The receivers would finally be moving in, and the TD Bank would be getting some of the money it was owed. Bob and his fellow workers would have to keep looking for jobs, and most of those jobs would not provide the same pay and benefits that the union jobs at the paper mill once did. But they didn't have any regrets about what they did. They didn't see it as a futile gesture. That's because the Thorold occupation was all about a tradition as old as the labour movement – helping someone else, and standing up for what's right.

The whole story was a roller-coaster ride of emotions, hopes raised, dashed, raised again. On Friday, October 15, 1999, CEP rep Mike Lambert was finally able to call Bob Browning, the president of the local at the mill. There was good news. He had just heard from CEP's Ontario vice-president, and Cec Makowski had told him that one of the companies that had been kicking the tires had finally agreed. There was new money coming. The aging mill would be reopening within a year. Just as he was about to hang up the phone, Mike's beeper went off. It was Cec again. The deal was off.

That was when Mike and Bob and the rest of the group started to make some plans of their own. Mike headed down to the local Canadian Tire, where he bought four hundred feet of chain and had it cut into ten-foot lengths. He also picked up forty locks that weekend, instructing a locksmith to make a single key that would fit them all. When they arrived at the gate before dawn on Monday morning, the security guard recognized a lot of familiar faces. He was nearing the end of his shift and needed a break.

"Hey, I'm glad you guys are here. Keep an eye on the gate while I go to the washroom."

> **Within minutes the CEP members were in the plant. They locked all the doors and gates behind them. They spent twenty-six days and nights there, having meetings and painting the forklifts.**

Within minutes the CEP members were in the plant. They locked all the doors and gates behind them. They spent twenty-six days and nights there, having meetings and painting the forklifts. They did all the things necessary to keep the place in good running order, using huge monkey wrenches to turn over the machines manually, making sure that the bearings didn't develop flat spots that would add to any new operator's costs. They stretched a huge tarp over the floor, decorated it with a TD logo and a plump pig sitting on a pile of money bags, and hung it out the window: "Toronto Dominion Bank, $1.48 billion profit, What About Us?"

But what everyone really remembered about it all was the community support. Anyone who has ever been on strike will remember how grateful they were for all the free coffee and donuts that strangers bring to the picket line. The Thorold occupation was all about how a small community rallied to support one of CEP's militant actions. Restaurants supplied entire dinners, complete with wait staff. Hundreds of chicken wings and dozens of pizzas kept arriving. An elderly woman from a nearby seniors' building was curious about all the commotion. After she learned what was happening she arrived the next day with two huge pots of cabbage rolls.

Aside from the food and the endless goodwill messages, the mayor of Thorold was an important supporter of the effort to reopen the mill. There was never any question of police intervention.

THE GLOBE AND MAIL

▲ *The Thorold occupation was all about a tradition as old as the labour movement – helping someone else, and standing up for what's right.*

Employers and banks were again reminded that this was not an organization that would roll over and play dead when confronted with a challenge.

There were, however, lots of visitors, including CEP's founding president Don Holder, who returned to his hometown to offer his support and tell the workers how proud he was of what they were doing. Don got his start at the Thorold mill in the 1950s.

Mike Lambert recalled sitting around the dining-room table in the Northern Ontario town of Iroquois Falls as a boy, listening to Don and his father – a mill worker for forty-seven years and a union activist – swap stories. Mike figured that was how he ended up leading an illegal factory occupation.

▶

▲ *The CEP members who occupied the plant knew they had done everything possible to back their union in its stubborn efforts to save the mill and the jobs. Rick Bedford celebrates the end of the Thorold occupation.*

"I would sit there and listen," he recalled. "I grew up in a family where you learned about moral responsibilities and social responsibilities. If somebody left us a legacy, if somebody fought for good wages and benefits, then we have to leave that legacy for our children."

Despite all the community support the workers received, the occupation was no holiday. The occupiers never left the plant, never saw their families. The tension level remained high as the days turned into weeks. It seemed that every Wednesday a successful sale had been finalized and every Thursday the deal evaporated. In the end, a purchase agreement was finalized and the occupiers left the plant to be greeted by a bagpiper and the cheers of a thousand people from the community. It was an emotional moment, and more than a few tears were shed. But by the following spring it had become apparent that this was another deal that would not go through.

Still, the CEP members who occupied the plant had no regrets. They knew that they had done everything they possibly could to back their union in its stubborn efforts to save the mill and the jobs that were so important in Thorold. Along with the CEP logo, something else was inscribed on their insiders' jackets: "We Made A Difference."

The occupation also said something about the militant spirit of a union that was just eight years old when the occupation began. Employers and banks were again reminded that this was not an organization that would roll over and play dead when confronted with a challenge. CEP members were again assured that the union would do everything possible when they needed help.

"When all other avenues have been closed there are still opportunities to achieve a successful outcome by taking a different approach, even if it's illegal," said Cec Makowski. "People often say, 'Hey, that's illegal.' I often say, 'Yeah, it's illegal. But your forefathers did a lot of illegal things for the labour movement.' In fact, unions themselves were illegal at one time." ▵

industry decided to pay additional dues of two hours a week to support the strike – around $50 a week per member. This brought strike pay up to $400. But it was more than a paperworker effort. Things had changed since 1975. (Frank Tremblett was glad when he lost a $20 bet with then Atlantic vice-president Elmo Whittom. Unlike Frank, Elmo had been confident that they would get regular financial support from other paper locals.)

"We spent a lot of money and brought all our people together," said Clément L'Heureux, executive vice-president of CEP for Quebec. "Imagine if the paper sector hadn't been helped by people in communications and people in energy to build up our strike fund. We would never have been able to confront a company like Abitibi and support men and women in a five-month strike."

Third, the Abitibi strike showed that workers in small communities are quite willing and most able to face down an aggressive employer.

The men in suits who toil in Abitibi's Toronto executive suites are no doubt aware of the difference between walking a picket line in July and walking one in January. But they do not live in the remote communities where the wealth that pays for those suits and suites gets produced. The value of long, warm summer days, when you can get a chance to fish, play golf, or just relax at your camp, is not as clear to them as it is to papermakers and millwrights in Shawinigan or Iroquois Falls or Grand Falls.

There are, of course, a certain number of people in forest-based towns who like to dress up in carpet-like winter gear, jump on their snowmobiles, and go ice fishing. Some may enjoy cross-country skiing. But, for the most part, outdoor time means summertime. The weather was fine in the summer of 1998. People took the opportunity presented by the strike and the strike pay to relax. They had lots of time to enjoy the great outdoors. Much golf got played, as the workers shaved away their handicaps.

▼ *The long Abitibi strike showed that workers in small communities are willing and able to face down a big, aggressive employer.*

W. SAUNDERS

Rat trap, 1994. ►
An early example of cross-sector support within CEP. Local 2000 media workers supported CEP paperworkers on strike against MacMillan Bloedel's use of rat unions to undercut industry standards.

"It was a strike, but it was also a festival. Instead of solidarity crumbling, the effect was the opposite."

Of course, back in town the picket lines stayed solid. As Philippe Hanna fondly recalled, the strike in Shawinigan took on a festive air. Local businesses and individuals were generous. Chinese food and pizza arrived regularly at a strike trailer that had a regular water supply compliments of a friendly neighbour. No one in the neighbourhood had any objection to the impromptu concerts put on by strikers at the Belgo mill, where there are a good number of amateur musicians. In fact, the neighbours joined in the singing.

"The guys had fun. We even installed a swimming pool," Philippe said. He recalled how things got better as the weeks turned into months. "It was a strike, but it was also a festival. Instead of solidarity crumbling, the effect was the opposite."

Well into the strike's third month, a company that had gone on the offensive, confidently feeling that it could break the pattern and weaken the new union, began to suffer the effects of blowback. It had certainly never intended to make the striking locals stronger and more determined by trying to push them around. By Labour Day the employer began to sue for peace, but the CEP negotiators were in no hurry to settle. They went to meet with the company in Montreal, where they discussed the process by which they might agree to return to the table. But, they told the suddenly impatient company, the CEP national convention was coming up. The union leaders and staff headed off for the meetings in Vancouver, while the other members strolled the picket lines and the fairways.

Returning to the table, the union began a bargaining session that lasted well into October. The momentum, as they say on the hockey broadcasts, had shifted. There was no more talk about destroying pattern bargaining. CEP issues were on the table and the union was in a sufficiently strong position that the negotiating team decided on a strategic move. They took an Abitibi offer back to the membership, which, as they had predicted, rejected it soundly. It was only a matter a time before they returned once again to Montreal and within a week had hammered out a final agreement. The negotiators departed with an offer that they could recommend to the membership: 22.5 per cent over six years, with pension improvements. But the real gain was recognition of the Abitibi group in these negotiations and the next round of negotiations. The word "capitulation" was heard at more than a few of the ratification meetings.

The value of pattern bargaining

THE WAY MAX MICHAUD SEES IT, pattern bargaining is what gives wage stability to the workers in the energy and paper industries. If Abitibi had been able to break CEP's pattern-setting ability, it would have meant that a company's less-profitable plants would pay lower wages than its stronger operations. Pattern bargaining allows the workers to benefit from the same economies of scale that their big employers enjoy from having a number of production facilities. "If you don't negotiate a pattern deal, you have no chance of doing that," said Max, CEP's Atlantic vice-president.

Frank Tremblett of Grand Falls put it succinctly: "If we went out and just shut down one of these mills, they'd laugh at us."

It's an issue that gets at the heart of the most important trade union ideal: united we stand, divided we fall. An injury to one is an injury to all. The feeble strength of one. The phrases are familiar, but no less true today than when they were first coined. Even the commonplace term "collective bargaining" suggests that workers succeed not as individuals but as a united group. Similarly, corporations and the special interest groups they fund are always trying to get us to see ourselves as individual "taxpayers" looking out for Number One, not as citizens with much in common.

This tendency gets played out in Canada's industrial relations system, where the deck is stacked against labour. Unlike many European countries, where unions bargain on a national and industry-wide basis with many employers at once, Canada forces most workers to deal with separate provincial labour boards even when they work in nationwide industries and companies. CEP locals at Abitibi in Ontario had to deal with that province's anti-union regulations – a challenge not faced by locals in Quebec, where the

> "If we went out and just shut down one of these mills, they'd laugh at us."
> • FRANK TREMBLETT

Pattern, or national, bargaining is a good idea for the same reason that collective bargaining makes sense – it increases the union's ability to negotiate better contracts.

rules are more balanced. And this was in a situation in which CEP at least had enterprise-based bargaining. If Canada had industry-based bargaining instead of an individually oriented system, unions would be better placed to deal with companies that are getting bigger and bigger.

"This system leaves the economic elite with a monopoly on the big picture," concluded a 1990 book on the Energy and Chemical Workers Union. "It leaves unions with scrambled pieces of a jigsaw."

Like its predecessor unions, CEP has consistently linked the pieces of the bargaining jigsaw by emphasizing the need for bargaining at One Big Table. It has also combined theory with practice, just as it did during the Abitibi strike. CEP maintains a national energy bargaining program. The large-scale telco bargaining units group together large numbers of workers working for a common employer; and CEP's efforts to secure national bargaining for CEP locals at CanWest-Global television stations were aimed directly at countering the effects of a corporate plan based on centralization and downsizing. If the logic of capital has it that corporate decisions are taken in one place, it only makes sense for the employees affected by those decisions to sit down with the employer in one place. Pattern, or national, bargaining is a good idea for the same reason that collective bargaining makes sense – it increases the union's ability to negotiate better contracts.

Fortunately, CEP's defence of pattern bargaining in the Abitibi dispute allowed its members to continue to enjoy the benefits of a strategy that, as Cec Makowski described it, cuts across "their linguistic differences, their cultural differences, and their regional differences." It is an advantage that requires a commitment that is often tricky to maintain but always worth the effort.

Frank Tremblett, a Newfoundlander born and bred, only learned after several years of trips to Montreal and Toronto and many days of wage policy conferences and bargaining sessions how to understand what trade unionists from Quebec were saying. It's not that the simultaneous interpretation was faulty. He kept losing track of what the representatives from Grand-Mère and Beaupré were saying. It finally dawned on him that he had to teach himself to look down at the table and concentrate on what he was hearing.

"If I looked up at the person who was at the microphone, I'd watch his lips and I'd lose the translation in the ear," Frank said. At the same time he recognized that it was all as difficult for the French-speaking people as it was for him.

The Newfoundlander made no comment on any difficulty that English speakers from Ontario might have in understanding people who hailed from Dark Cove or Black Tickle. He did, however, recall an incident during a strike

K. NEWMAN

◀ *Workers in Shawinigan and the other Abitibi mills returned to work with a wage increase and pension improvements. But the real victory was the recognition of pattern bargaining.*

in 1980. A tense bargaining session had just ended. There was a done deal and negotiators on both sides of the table were dead tired. But, as president of his local, Frank could not accept a clause that would have deprived temporary workers at the Grand Falls mill of work for the next year. As the company began discussing the schedule for restarting the mills, he got up to explain his problem. He said it didn't matter what the other mills did, Grand Falls was staying down. It wasn't easy because he knew that everyone had figured the package was wrapped up.

The room fell silent until a delegate from Chandler, Quebec, approached the microphone. Even though the man spoke very little English, he wanted to make his point clear, so he did his best. In any case, his message was brief and to the point. "If Brother Frank don't work, we don't work."

It took Abitibi only a few brief minutes to agree to meet the demands from Grand Falls.

"Even when I talk about that today, I get the cold shivers," Frank said. "Because I didn't believe we could support each other like that, being from different walks of life. I'll remember that till I go to my grave."

CHAPTER SIX

Gaspésia and the preservation of Chandler

THESE PLACES ARE SPRINKLED across the country apparently at random, as though someone tossed a handful of pebbles onto the map. They have a few things in common, aside from being out in the backcountry a long way from the centres of financial and political power.

They are close to the forest frontier because that's where the timber and the ore are. They are close to the ocean because that's where the fish are, or were. Some of these places exist as virtual ghost towns. Tottering headframes of abandoned mines rise above the timberline, or tumbledown outport docks are left abandoned on shore. A few rotting boilers and rusty flywheels provide evidence of an old sawmill.

Some of the places, though, are still going strong. Others exist in a twilight world, uncertain about even the immediate future. If a town owes its prosperity to the pulp and paper boom that started after the turn of the last century, chances are you can find a neighbourhood where the houses are grand, set apart from each other on generous lots with mature trees. These leafy suburbs were home to the mill manager, the woodland manager, the

▲ *Without the active intervention of CEP and the Fonds de solidarité FTQ, the fate of Gaspésia Paper would have mirrored that of the cod fishery, shut down in the early 1990s. An FTQ demonstration in support of Chandler.*

By 2002 Chandler's Gaspésia Paper mill was standing silent. The rickety gate to the woodlands department was secured not by a lock but by a chain welded to the fence.

J. SWIFT

financial manager. Perhaps they had their own golf course, property of the company, for the exclusive use of the bosses.

Chandler is one of these places.

Quebec's Gaspé Peninsula once had a fabulous fishery. Edmond Sirois, seventy, is the long-time mayor of nearby Grande-Rivière and chair of the council of mayors of the Rocher-Percé region. When I talked to him in early 2002, he recalled a hundred local boats parading out into the Gulf. In the old days before refrigeration and factory trawlers, the peninsula's wide beaches, steady winds, and abundant sunshine made the Gaspé a perfect place for drying cod. Its thick stands of white spruce and its fast-flowing rivers promised jobs for loggers and papermakers in the pulp and paper industry.

By 2002 Chandler's Gaspésia Paper mill was standing silent. The rickety gate to the woodlands department was secured not by a lock but by a chain welded to the fence. A few rusting grapple loaders and bulldozers sat near an orange pickup with an Abitibi-Price logo on its door. Three tank cars sat abandoned on a railway spur near the mill, where more than five hundred CEP members once worked. Up on the other side of the mill, where the bosses lived, weeds were pushing up between the crumbling slabs of concrete sidewalk. The nearby golf course, now open to the general public, had recently been expanded to eighteen holes – one of the many projects created to provide work for unemployed mill workers.

It was, all in all, a bleak scene. The town of Chandler, population 4,000, had been hit hard when Abitibi closed the Gaspésia mill in 1999. People left, stores closed, and small businesses dried up. It's a pattern common to the Gaspé, where they often talk about how many young people have become "exiled." When they get to Montreal, the economic deportees tend to talk proudly of their Gaspésian roots, but they don't often make plans to return. The region is well known as the poorest in Quebec. Edmond Sirois explained that when Gaspésia stopped operating, it was more like a regional shutdown than a mill closure. The ripple effect was strong in a region where the official unemployment rate was already running at 24 per cent.

Still, according to the mayor, things are now looking up. "You should have seen people's faces light up when the machinery entered the yard last week," he said with a grin. "I was one of those who didn't think it would ever reopen. But the union played a crucial role. Not only did it buy the mill, it influenced the government to invest as well."

Without the active intervention of CEP and the Fonds de solidarité FTQ (the Solidarity Fund administered by the Fédération des travailleurs et travailleuses du Québec, the FTQ), the fate of Gaspésia Paper would have mirrored that of the cod fishery, shut down in the early 1990s, and Noranda's copper mining operation at Murdochville in the Gaspé interior, closed in 2002.

"We've got that fighting spirit," said Pierre-Suzor Coté, one of the CEP members who worked on the campaign to save the mill. "We want to stay in our place and we want to save it. Here in the Gaspé we're people of the sea, the forest. This will be a turning point for our region."

Organizing in a period of uncertainty

WHEN CEP MEMBERS at every Abitibi-Consolidated mill in Eastern Canada went on strike in 1998, there was already some unease in Chandler about the future of the town's main employer.

◀ *A few rusting grapple loaders and bulldozers sat near an orange pickup with an Abitibi-Price logo on its door.*

J. SWIFT

Pieces on the game board of globalization

THE MEN IN SUITS who control the industry move paper mills and entire companies around like pieces on a Monopoly board. The outfit that is now called Abitibi-Consolidated is a case in point.

For many years the Gaspésia mill was owned by the company of William Price and Sons, formed originally by Englishman William Price. Some people call Price the "Father of the Saguenay" because he became rich in the nineteenth century by selling timber from the Quebec forests granted to him by the British government. His business eventually passed into the hands of his grandson Sir William Price, who cashed in on the U.S. newsprint boom of the early twentieth century.

The younger Price was an ardent imperialist, knighted for his services to the British in South Africa. When he was killed in an accident while inspecting his Saguenay timber empire in 1924, the event was marked by big headlines and an outpouring of sentimental eulogies from the rich and powerful. In those years there was not a single Quebec watershed from the Saguenay to the Gatineau where the portages and shorelines were not dotted with crude wooden crosses. Carved with the initials of a logger who had been drowned or crushed as he tried to free a log jam in the springtime river drive, these were the lonely memorials to those killed making sure that the woodyards at the downstream mills were full by June.

In the late 1970s the Price Co. Ltd. joined forces with the rival Abitibi interests to form Abitibi-Price. After passing through the hands of Toronto's Reichmann family, in 1997 the company that likes to call itself the largest newsprint producer in the world merged with Stone-Consolidated, itself the product of a merger between the Stone paper interests in the United States and another old Canadian company, Consolidated-Bathurst.

Although the company's profits came to nearly a billion dollars between 1997 and 2000, Abitibi-Consolidated continued to neglect the Gaspésia mill.

Although the company's profits came to nearly a billion dollars between 1997 and 2000, Abitibi-Consolidated continued to neglect the Gaspésia mill. It spent its time and money not by investing in the mills and communities that were the basis of its prosperity but in an effort to become a bigger global player. In 1998 it invested $U.S. 250 million in a newsprint mill in Snowflake, Arizona. In 1999 it entered a joint venture with Scandinavian and Asian capital to create the Pan Asia Paper Company, the biggest newsprint operation in the Asia-Pacific region. In 2000, in a controversial move, Abitibi-Consolidated acquired Quebec's Donohue Inc. in a $7 billion cash and stock deal. △

People in the community were aware of the difficulties that the plant faced. Word got around that the PCMB pulping process that the company (then Abitibi-Price) had installed in the mid-1980s had never worked as well as company executives had believed it would. The machinery could not handle the white spruce that was the principal fibre input, which forced the company to supplement the recipe with kraft pulp and recycled newsprint. The workers also reported that the mill was increasingly a haywire operation suffering from lack of investment by a corporate owner apparently not much interested in its future. The plant lacked resources and the employees often had to scramble to keep things running smoothly. Sometimes quality suffered and the product was hard to sell to North American publishers, forcing Abitibi to sell it to less demanding buyers in Latin America.

Gaspésia Paper had become the poor cousin in a big corporate family. In 1995 Abitibi revealed its strategy of dividing its mills into "cornerstone" and "non-cornerstone" operations. The company paid big money to consultants from McKinsey and Company to figure this one out. (Corporate managers, particularly those who have trouble keeping in touch with their own operations, love to hire outside consultants who have acquired glossy reputations.) Despite being relatively new – its paper machines were only twenty years old – the Chandler mill was a high-cost producer. It had no dedicated hydro-electricity supply from a dam of its own.

After a strong earnings period in the industry in 1995, a downturn began. In 1997 Abitibi-Price merged with Stone-Consolidated to form

◀ *Some 4,500 people crammed the Chandler arena to hear speeches of solidarity and famous performers such as Laurence Jalbert and Nelson Mainville.*

Some said that to go on strike against a mill that was not doing all that well to begin with was to court disaster.

Abitibi-Consolidated, or "Abitibi-Consol" as it is known in Chandler. The new company's first annual report let it be known that it was thinking of permanent closure as a means of dealing with the mills that it had decided had not made the grade as cornerstones of its expanding corporate structure. In 1998 the rumour mill in Chandler began to work overtime. That year the Gaspésia workers joined CEP at other Abitibi mills in going on strike to defend their long-established right to bargain as one big union rather than allow the company to gain the upper hand by dealing with them one mill at a time.

In a region with lots of poverty, a strike by workers who make $25 an hour and have good pensions and fringe benefits is not always popular with everyone. According to Denis Luce, president of the papermakers local at Gaspésia, many people in the community criticized the mill workers for being "spoiled." Some said that to go on strike against a mill that was not doing all that well to begin with was to court disaster.

In the face of pressure from some quarters of the community, the workers maintained their solidarity over five long months on the picket line. They knew that they were on strike not against the Gaspésia mill but against a huge transnational corporation that, should it get its way, would be able to pick off weaker locals and wring concessions from them. They knew that their good wages and benefits had not come from a head office located in Montreal's Sun Life Building. Abitibi was no charitable organization. The workers' gains – as well as the gains in every other mill in Eastern Canada that provided exactly the same wages – had been achieved through a solid common front of union locals and, when necessary, strike action.

Of course, not everyone felt that the workers at Gaspésia had it easy. Mario Grenier, financial manager of the Centre local de développement du Rocher-Percé, was well aware that when unions sit down with the employer at a single table they stand to make good gains. "The teachers in Paspébiac are paid the same as those in Montreal," he pointed out. "That's because of pattern bargaining."

Community mental health worker Johanne Becu recalled that during her father Camille's thirty years in the wood room at the mill he had always told his friends and family that one day it would close. It would have little to do with what the union said or did. It became a regular theme around the dinner table. When people told him not to be such a pessimist, he would simply shrug and point out that the wood had to come from farther away each year and that the company and the government were neglecting reforestation.

In any case, the big strike of 1998 ended when Abitibi retreated from its attempt to break pattern bargaining. The workers at Chandler joined the rest of the CEP locals from Fort Frances to Grand Falls in returning to work that fall. Meanwhile, Abitibi, the Quebec government, and various companies that said they were interested in the plant (or perhaps its cutting rights) had been meeting to discuss Gaspésia's future. The closed-door negotiations involved the premier and the president of the company. Something was in the works.

But, as it turned out, no deal was reached and the winter of 1999 proved to be one of the most sombre that Chandler had ever experienced. Even as the negotiations proceeded, Abitibi shut down one of the two newsprint machines. The CEP organized a demonstration that filled the streets. In June 1999 the company shut the other paper machine. In late October came the final blow. Without giving any advance notice Abitibi boss John Weaver flew into town, announced that the mill was closing for good, and left as quickly as he had arrived. People in Chandler were shocked.

Johanne Becu, who referred to the whole period of gnawing uncertainty that followed as "the crisis," recalled that on October 28 people were walking around the town's shopping centre in stunned silence, as if a close family member had just died. "All of a sudden there was nothing. It was like the end of our world."

The crisis lasted for over two years, during which time the CEP activists in Chandler worked on a number of fronts. They organized a train trip to the rainy streets of Montreal to keep the pressure on Abitibi and the media

... continued on page 82

◀ *The crisis lasted for over two years. Chandler workers demonstrated many times, in the rain and the snow, in the heat and the cold, to save both their mill and the Gaspé economy.*

79

The saving of St. Marys Paper

WORKERS IN SAULT STE. MARIE have a record of expressing their opinions directly. In 1903 promoter Francis Clergue shut the doors of his steel mill while still owing his employees several months' back pay. The enraged workers took over the company office and rioted in the streets of the town. The government was forced to dispatch four hundred militiamen from Toronto, along with $250,000 to pay the back wages.

Clergue had financed the steel mill as well as what later became St. Marys Paper, the first Canadian pulp mill to be located close to hydro power and vast tracts of spruce forest. A hundred years later, the aging newsprint mill had come through some troubled times, and the union came up with a plan to save the mill by exchanging shares in the company for a temporary cut in pay. It was CEP activist Brad Jourdin's job to convince an anxious membership in four different locals that the union was on the right track. At the time he ended up being on the receiving end of some rather direct comments. "You take those fucking shares and shove them up your ass," someone told him.

In the end no one was cursing Brad out. Instead the workers were calculating when they should retire and pick up between $150,000 and $200,000 cash money, tax free, in exchange for their shares — on top of their regular pensions and, of course, the dividend cheques. By 2001 the workers were back at full pay, having regained what they had given up in wages.

The CEP-brokered plan to save the mill and virtually all of its 420 jobs was but one of a string of similar successes scored by the union within a few years of its formation, from Gaspésia in Chandler to Provincial Paper in Thunder Bay and, before that, a landmark victory in Kapuskasing, Ont. "St. Marys is still a raving success," said CEP secretary-treasurer André Foucault, a veteran of the successful fight to save the mill in Kapuskasing.

It was a success that had taken a lot of hard work and dedication. For Brad Jourdin, who had spent eighteen years as a welder by the time the owner declared bankruptcy in 1993, it was an extremely difficult period. Of course, when your job is on the line in a town where unemployment is already high and the steel mill always seems to be in trouble, you tend to be sceptical of new ideas. Some members thought that Brad and the other union activists were concocting a scam. Most thought that the mill was doomed to close no matter what CEP did.

"I really took a lot of shit-kicking along the way," Brad recalled. "I had a lot of nights when I didn't sleep." What he did was just keep telling

> The CEP-brokered plan to save the mill and virtually all of its 420 jobs was but one of a string of similar successes scored by the union within a few years of its formation.

▲ *"I had a lot of nights when I didn't sleep," Brad recalled. He just kept telling himself that they were doing the right thing. "That's how I got along." Brad Jourdin demonstrates in St. Catharines, Ont., May Day 1998.*

himself that they were doing the right thing. "That's how I got along."

The backing of the NDP government of the day was crucial, but it still took a year and a half to come up with an agreement. A new owner would refinance the old plant and transform it into a mill that would produce semi-gloss paper for catalogues and magazines. CEP got board representation and something called "ownership over fundamental decisions." That means that if the company wanted to take profits from the mill in the Sault and invest them in a mill that would compete in the same market, the union could veto the proposal, even though it only holds a minority on the board.

There were other changes at St. Marys Paper. Everyone working in the mill had an orientation session in which they learned directly from the sales staff about who would be buying their new paper products and why. People who had never left their own departments toured the mill to get an overview of how the place would be working. Union members also sat on the hiring committees that chose new mill managers, including the head of industrial relations.

After serving as a steward, guard, recording secretary, president, and vice-president of his local, Brad is as familiar as anyone with the life of a union activist. He has learned when to try to settle a dispute before it gets written up. He's suspicious of what CEP president Brian Payne calls "the flavour-of-the-month work regimes that are being foisted on us like never before." And he knows that local leaders who stay in close touch with the members and always take time to stop and talk are still likely to hear a few choice words from the rank and file: "Listen! Don't forget that you work for me."

Only now, the CEP members at St. Marys are also working for themselves. ▵

"We knew it was a big company without any heart," said Mario Grenier. "That was like me selling you a gas station and saying 'It's yours now. But you can't sell any gas.'"

spotlight on the plight not only of the Gaspésia mill but also of the entire Gaspé region. There were street demonstrations in Chandler. Another series of quiet, behind-the-scene negotiations began, this time at the initiative of CEP and its close allies in the Quebec Federation of Labour's big Fonds de solidarité. It helped that CEP's executive vice-president for Quebec, Clément L'Heureux, was on the board of the fund and the executive of the FTQ.

Within six weeks of Abitibi's announcement Pierre-Suzor Coté had organized the *Grand soulèvement gaspésien*. Some 4,500 people crammed the Chandler arena to hear speeches of solidarity and see famous performers such as Laurence Jalbert and Nelson Mainville, who hailed from the region and returned to play for free in support of the cause. Suzor was especially pleased that so many young people showed up to stand and cheer beneath CEP's familiar triangular symbol. Their future in the region was at stake. While he was arranging the hugely successful event, Suzor had thousands of big yellow stickers printed up: "Abitibi-Consolidated has betrayed Gaspésiens!'

That was only the half of it. Several months after the CEP's representatives began their negotiations to find new money and a new operator for Gaspésia, they found out that Abitibi would be happy to sell its Chandler property. But there was one condition. It would only sell if the buyer of the newsprint mill would agree not to use it to produce newsprint for ten years.

"We knew it was a big company without any heart," said Mario Grenier. "That was like me selling you a gas station and saying 'It's yours now. But you can't sell any gas.'"

Within six weeks of ▶ *Abitibi's announcement that the mill was closing for good, Pierre-Suzor Coté had organized the* Grand soulèvement gaspésien.

This condition made the whole affair more complicated. It would have been tricky enough to find a new owner and arrange financing for a mill whose pulping process was a chronic headache. The cost of installing a new thermo-mechanical pulping (TMP) system and refurbishing the newsprint machines would have been in the neighbourhood of $150 million, whereas converting the whole process to produce a different kind of paper would probably be much more expensive: as it turned out, three times more expensive. Yet in the end CEP pulled it off with more than a little help from its friends.

"We had a great deal of solidarity inside the union," said Denis Luce, a twenty-seven-year veteran of the mill who would emerge as a key leader during the crisis. He acted as a liaison between the local and the leadership in Quebec and Montreal.

Raising the money and finding a buyer added up to a huge challenge. Keeping the workers together so that the mill would have an intact workforce when it reopened was another problem. It required the combined efforts of the CEP leadership in Ottawa and Montreal together with that of the Quebec labour movement as a whole.

"We had people supporting us," said Denis. "At the time, we had Fred Pomeroy as president, Clément L'Heureux and Henri Massé from the FTQ. It would have been totally impossible without them."

The crisis and the Solidarity Fund

AT FIRST IT DID NOT SOUND like a lucky number for Denis Luce, Pierre-Suzor Coté, Claude Blais, and all the rest of the CEP activists who worked on the campaign to save the Gaspésia mill: 1313. But that was what you got when you added up Local 455 and Local 858, the two unions that had represented the production workers and the papermakers respectively in Chandler.

Getting the two groups to merge was more a matter of hard work than luck, because, as anyone who has ever worked in a unionized paper mill knows, there are sometimes divisions. Sandy Beckingham, president of a CEP local across the Baie de Chaleur in Dalhousie, N.B., explained that papermakers tend to be "clannish," a standoffish breed unto themselves. Merven Lucas retired from the Gaspésia mill during the closure, after many years as a local union leader. He said that production workers, especially in the skilled trades, sometimes get jealous because papermakers who have less formal training than they do often make more money.

Nevertheless the Gaspésia closure drew the factions together. Sometimes 350 people would come out for a union meeting, something unheard of in days

The $4.6 billion Solidarity Fund is one of the biggest pools of capital in Quebec. It's also the only one controlled directly by trade unionists. The fund invests in jobs close to home and specializes in helping troubled workplaces turn things around.

When Henri Massé of the FTQ, chair of the Solidarity Fund, and CEP's Clément L'Heureux, who sits on the fund's board, began to make their calls, the key people in the Quebec government took notice.

gone by, except perhaps at contract ratification time. Not that the creation of Local 1313 was without problems. The anxiety of the period created new conflicts and brought old ones to the surface as different factions pushed different agendas. Emotions ran high due to the uncertainties of the high-stakes game that got played out over the course of two years. People were desperate and grabbed at any straw that anyone offered. Still, Denis Luce found that it was a positive experience on a very basic level. "I had best friends before the events who unfortunately became worst enemies. There were also people I knew in a cursory manner who became the best friends and the best supporters that I could have wished for."

CEP's success at Chandler had little to do with luck when it came to dealing with the big picture. That took big money, money available in the form of the Quebec Federation of Labour's Solidarity Fund. As they say, money talks.

It is safe to say that, when it comes to dealing with government, some voices are louder than others. It's called "access," and many organizations pay top dollar for the services of lobbyists who promise to provide it. When bankers and large corporations want the ear of a particular minister – or even the prime minister – they have less difficulty having their calls returned than, say, a group promoting the rights of disabled people. So when Henri Massé of the FTQ, chair of the Solidarity Fund, and CEP's Clément L'Heureux, who sits on the fund's board, began to make their calls, the key people in the Quebec government took notice.

That's in good measure because the $4.6 billion fund is one of the biggest pools of capital in Quebec. It's also the only one controlled directly by trade unionists. The fund invests in jobs close to home and specializes in helping troubled workplaces turn things around. Although there are labour-sponsored funds in other provinces (invest and you get a regular RRSP deduction *and* a big tax credit), there's nothing anywhere else so big or so well-known among the public at large. Nearly half a million people in Quebec hold shares in the fund.

The fund has been instrumental in providing support for 93,000 jobs. As it turned out, the purchase of the Gaspésia mill was one of the biggest projects that the fund had ever undertaken.

It took over a year to conclude the negotiations. In the course of the talks the union representatives learned that Abitibi intended to make it more expensive to turn the mill around with its no-newsprint clause, but they figured they had no choice but to go ahead. The future of Chandler and indeed of the whole region was at stake. In December 2000, fourteen months after Abitibi walked away from Gaspésia, the fund bought the mill for $35 million. Before signing, the fund and CEP did their homework. They were reasonably sure that they could bring in enough public and private capital to reopen the mill. But it would still take an additional year of tricky negotiations to finalize the deal, during which time the rumour mill even claimed that the fund had not in fact bought the mill.

In the meantime, employment insurance benefits for the Gaspésia workers had run out. While Denis Luce handled liaison tasks with the people in Quebec City, Montreal, and Ottawa as well as the media work – the Chandler struggle became a *cause célèbre* in Quebec – it was up to Pierre-Suzor Coté and a group of backroom organizers to make sure that as many people as possible got work and stayed in the Gaspé. The government had to be persuaded that what had happened was the equivalent of 50,000 jobs disappearing all at once in Montreal, that the minimum-wage projects that are so often a staple for poor people in the country's poor regions would not keep the mill workers from joining the Gaspé's economic exiles in Montreal. CEP was instrumental in organizing a series of $12 an hour projects. The golf course got nine new holes. A new union hall took shape from an old Hydro Québec building. Snowmobile trails were established and upgraded. The residential-care facility of the community mental health centre was outfitted with new furniture.

Which is not to say that the crisis did not take a big toll on people in Chandler and vicinity. Over her years of working on mental health problems, Johanne Becu had developed an understanding of the hidden undercurrents of life in the area. Although poverty is familiar to too many Gaspésiens, she noticed a new kind of poverty after the mill closed. It was hidden in houses with $40,000 jeeps parked outside. Some people were so attached to the appearances and trappings of success that they started to cut back on heat and food in order to meet payments. Others borrowed from their retired parents, who chose to do without rather than say no.

She explained the psychological manifestations of the crisis as she helped a tall, shy-looking man in his thirties with a bag of groceries. Canned soup, bananas, spaghetti, bread: the end of the month. "I've had women say to me, 'I left this morning and my husband was sitting staring at the floor and when I came back in the afternoon he was still sitting there. He hadn't eaten. I don't know if he had even moved.'"

The depression that had hung like an ocean fog over the town had begun to lift by August 2001, when it became clear that the union effort was paying dividends in the form of commitments from Ottawa and Quebec. The federal government committed $80 million in loans to the project, and the province came up with a total of $153 million in grants, loans, and training money. It did not hurt that the riding was represented by government members in both

"This outcome can be attributed to workers and their union leader, Denis Luce, whose name will forever be linked to solidarity."
• QUEBEC PREMIER BERNARD LANDRY

Pierre-Suzor Coté ▶ *was an organizer of the campaign to save the Gaspésia mill. The sign used to say Abitibi-Consolidated. Now it reads "Propriété des Gaspésiens."*

capitals, but Local 1313 could still legitimately claim that its success was due more to hard work than good luck. Another good sign was the decision by the forest products company Tembec to come in as managing partner in a three-cornered partnership that included the Solidarity Fund (with a 50 per cent interest in the project) and SGF-Rexfor, a government-owned firm.

In all it would cost $465 million to completely refurbish the Gaspésia mill, transforming it into a TMP mill producing 200,000 tonnes of high-gloss coated paper using the latest Scandinavian technology. The new high-value-added facility, to be opened in 2004, would employ 260 people. Before the deal was finally announced Local 1313 had negotiated a long-term contract with Tembec. Although Gaspésia would not be employing as many people as it had when its two newsprint machines were running full out, older workers like Merven Lucas, with his thirty-six years of service, had taken their retirement and a new wallboard mill just up Highway 132 in Grande-Rivière would employ another 150 people, also members of CEP.

At the time of the announcement of the new project, Quebec premier Bernard Landry presented his assessment of what had happened. "This outcome can be attributed to workers and their union leader, Denis Luce, whose name will forever be linked to solidarity."

Taking ownership

FOR THE TWO LONG YEARS that it took to get things back on track in Chandler, Merven Lucas and a handful of other Gaspésia workers would gather at the CEP hall to chew over the latest developments and speculate about the future. Denis Luce credits this group with providing the backbone that the local union needed to see the new project through. He described Merven as the mentor who taught him all about trade unionism. "We'd sit around here every morning and encourage Denis," Merven said in his quiet, matter-of-fact way. "We needed to stay together. It was the only way to get it done."

Merven served as president of the Gaspésia papermakers back in the 1970s. They "were always ready for a fight," one of the most militant groups when it came to dealing with Abitibi. Still, the crisis offered Merven the chance to meet people he had never really talked to in all the time he had spent at the mill. He worked with the Employee Assistance Plan, whose services were more in demand than ever. He also watched as people began to drift away from the region – especially those who needed more money than the temporary projects could offer or who gave up hope. It's easier for skilled trades to find jobs, harder for the papermakers who are labourers when they get away from the paper machine. His brother spent some time in Montreal before heading home because he could not bear to hear his daughter crying over the phone, asking him if he was ever coming back.

"Twenty years ago there was money around here," recalled Merven, who put his children through college with his union wages. "People were fishing cod. The mill was running. There were people working in Murdochville."

Still, Merven is one of the people who figured that the writing was on the wall for Gaspésia, at least under Abitibi's control. He thinks the globalizing multinational would simply have just kept running the Chandler mill into the ground, a bit of shop-floor reckoning that his former employer confirmed just as the restart deal was being finalized in 2001. Abitibi announced that it had decided to "clamp down even further on capital expenditures. We will limit our capex to below $300 million this year, or less than 50% of our expected depreciation levels ..."

The next spring Merven was driving up Rue Commercial. The mill takes up one side of Chandler's main street. He had made the trip ten thousand times in his thirty-six years at Gaspésia. He passed the church, Sacre Coeur de Marie, and l'École St-Joseph. La Taverne Cyr, where generations of men from the mill would gather over quart bottles of beer after work, had become Bistro Cyr and now welcomed women. Several storefronts stood empty. A tall crane, the symbol of hope that had moved in just before winter, stood in the mill yard.

"They were cleaning things up and they had some pumps working," he said. "I stopped my jeep and opened my window and listened to the noise. I said to myself, 'Jeez it's good to hear that. It's been quiet for three years.'"

Merven paused, chuckling quietly. "Now people will be able to stay here with their families."

Lucas Merven watched as people began to drift away from the region – especially those who needed more money than the temporary projects could offer or who gave up hope.

As he continued up the street he passed the sign beside the main access road to the mill. It used to say Abitibi-Consolidated. But someone had covered it up with a huge handmade map of the Gaspé Peninsula. A little paper mill symbol placed on the south coast highlighted Chandler. The new sign, big enough for anyone passing by to read, said *La Compagnie Gaspésia Ltée: Propriété des Gaspésiens.*

CHAPTER SEVEN

Forestry, climate change, and energy:
BUILDING NEW POLICIES

JUST AS CEP WAS BEING FORMED in 1992, British Columbia was being labelled the Brazil of the North because of its reckless forest practices. Global Warming had become as familiar a term as Globalization. The governments of the world were establishing an Intergovernmental Panel on Climate Change. The scientific panel was charged with the task of helping the world come to terms with climate chaos. Concern over the fate of the planet was reaching a peak.

The union's founding convention took place in the wake of the famous Earth Summit held in Rio de Janeiro that year (and therefore also known as the Rio Summit). The United Nations gathering was as notable for the number of non-governmental organizations (NGOs) that came together to challenge conventional notions of "sustainable development" as it was for the formal declarations produced by the official delegates.

A strong current among the environmentalists – particularly activists from the poor countries of the South – was that it was high time that notions like "justice" and "equality" percolated into the green movement. In the years since Rio, the flourishing anti-globalization movement has recognized that land

▲ *CEP seeks allies amongst activists who believe not in corporate globalization but in a world in which people gain control over the decisions that affect their lives.*

89

reform, women's rights, unjust trade relations, and poverty are green issues. Social justice is inseparable from environmental sustainability.

This was where CEP would seek its allies: among activists who shared the view that sustainable development was only a phrase used by public relations specialists to polish the image of mining and logging companies; who saw development in the same way as the CEP's Southern partners in Humanity Fund projects did; who believed not in corporate globalization but in a world in which people could gain control over the decisions that had an impact on their lives.

A national forest policy

THE CEP CUT ITS TEETH on forestry issues in British Columbia. Visitors to the B.C. regional office are greeted with posters, published by the province's broadly based environmental movement, displaying images of giant cedar trees. In 1991 an NDP government had been elected. People were sitting in trees to protest logging of this watershed or getting arrested to save that grizzly habitat, and the province set up a process that involved everyone concerned. The new union became heavily involved, learning a lot about the importance of understanding both technical issues and the politics of forestry. When the time came to develop a national forestry policy, CEP struck a committee of officers, rank and file board members, and staff. The idea was to take the time – a full year – to do it right.

It takes several human generations to grow a healthy forest, so forestry is a long-term undertaking. Because forestry is also very much a regional issue, the committee included representatives from each part of the country. The committee invited in professional foresters from each region so that the union would have expert assistance in coming up with an understanding of the complexities of natural versus artificial regeneration and the different types of forest tenure.

By the time the committee had met a half-dozen times, its members had become familiar with the issues: silviculture, biodiversity, forest management, the globalization of the trade in forest products. By the time its members had generated several drafts of the policy, they had taken ownership of the issue and were ready to take it on the road. Each region held workshops designed to promote a two-way flow of information, with committee members encouraging comments and suggestions.

The grassroots process succeeded in producing what the union had hoped for – a bold policy that confronted the real issues and did not avoid controversy. Above all, it did not fall into the trap of succumbing to job black-

In the years since Rio, the flourishing anti-globalization movement has recognized that land reform, women's rights, unjust trade relations, and poverty are green issues. Social justice is inseparable from environmental sustainability.

mail and getting into bed with the forest companies. It rejected the old industry line that clear-cutting mimics forest fires, and instead called for an end to excessive clear-cutting. It recommended the adoption of logging methods tailored to the realities of forest ecosystems, not to the cost of the wood delivered to the mill yard. CEP also argued for an end to two centuries of secrecy and private, behind-closed-door decisions by government and industry. Public policy on the public forest should "be made in democratic, public processes."

Perhaps most intriguingly, given the highly charged nature of debates on resource management, CEP stated bluntly that "tough environmental regulations do not harm the pulp and paper industry." What's more, while pointing out that it had different interests than industry, the union also underlined the need for "worker environmentalism" and recognized the environmental movement as its social partner.

CEP's only caveat centred on the need for give and take. It could not develop fruitful co-operation with environmental organizations that take actions affecting its members if those actions were taken without consultation or without taking the welfare of the members into account. The new national forest policy was adopted at CEP's convention in 2000.

Global warming and an energy policy

IN APRIL 2002 CEP waded into the heated debate on global climate change. Canada's energy union came out in support of the historic Kyoto Protocol, the international agreement committing countries to take the first slow steps towards reducing climate change by cutting greenhouse gas emissions. There was no choice. The world stood on the brink of environmental disaster.

Some of the world's most powerful energy corporations and their government supporters – Alberta's Ralph Klein had just insisted that breathing causes global warming – had a doomsday scenario of their own. They claimed that the Kyoto accord would lead to job loss and economic decline. CEP, having already passed a Just Transition policy, countered with a forceful argument that the time had come to switch to a sustainable economy.

Speaking in Ottawa when the union released a research report at the end of the month, CEP president Brian Payne made the union's position clear. "It doesn't have to be a question of jobs or the environment," he argued. "Clearly, we can have both."

"This is the kind of leadership and forward thinking we need," said David Suzuki, one of Canada's best-known environmentalists. "Instead of denying the need for change as other interest groups have done, the Communications,

... continued on page 95

▲ *CEP's forestry policy states bluntly that "tough environmental regulations do not harm the pulp and paper industry." It recommends the adoption of logging methods tailored to the realities of forest ecosystems, not to the cost of the wood delivered to the mill yard.*

The Fletcher Challenge strike

IT WAS THE LONGEST strike in the history of the Canadian pulp and paper industry. The CEP faced down the challenge of a global forest products giant intent on implementing a radical agenda that would have led to hundreds of lost jobs. It started in the summer of 1997 and lasted through the months when it rains sideways on Vancouver Island.

Over nine months later, neither side could claim complete victory. But while Fletcher Challenge had been forced out of Canada, four determined CEP locals – Local 630 (Campbell River papermakers), Local 1123 (Campbell River produc-tion workers), Local 1132 (Crofton papermakers) and Local 1092 (Mackenzie production workers) – which had voted 96 per cent in favour of meeting the challenge, remained, as did all the jobs. Along the way CEP became a stronger union, both locally and on a national basis. Moreover, the landmark strike against Fletcher Challenge was a co-operative effort with the Pulp, Paper and Woodworkers of Canada, Local 2, at Crofton.

" It was a classic example of pattern bargaining that held together from start to finish," said Brian Payne, Western Vice President and the CEP national officer responsible for the negotiations. "Fletcher Challenge were the pattern group and were supported by all the other Locals. After the strike, the pattern was successfully bargained in every location."

Soon after the strike started, the people of Campbell River were treated to full-page ads that showed a light bulb at the top of some stairs. They were asked why the workers could not climb the stairs to a good idea. That idea, said the company, was flexibility. The union moved quickly to counter that message with one of its own. The strike was about power, not flexibility.

"We were fighting to retain control over our work," said Greg Derouin, president of Local 630 in Campbell River at the time. "We didn't just sit back as we might have done in the past and wait for the industry pressure to force us back to the table."

CEP activists went to the press, appearing in the local media regularly and explaining that they had a collective agreement, not individual employment contracts. The issue, they said, had to do with an international company that was threatening a capital strike if it could not have its way with the province. They said the workers were well rooted in the community but Fletcher Challenge was interested in shareholder value, not social values.

The proactive tactics worked in Campbell River. The union members made sure that they touched

Fletcher Challenge, a multinational interested in share-holder value, not social values, was forced out of the country. CEP members, their workplaces, and communities remain unscathed.

Fletcher Challenge tried to counter union solidarity with ▶
threats of "international scabbing." CEP supporters in
Campbell River responded with a show of Canadian flags.

F. WILSON

all the bases, visiting the local service clubs to let
people know where they stood, and why.

"Getting the business community to be neutral
was a real achievement," Greg said. "They might
not have agreed totally with our position and they
might not have come to like unions, but they
understood we were trying to keep this transnational company from getting whatever it could
out of the community and leaving."

The four-hundred-dollar weekly strike pay and
the close attention that the local paid to meeting
with financial institutions meant that there wasn't
a single foreclosure in Campbell River during the
strike. Because it was a pattern-setting strike,
CEP's standard strike pay of $200 was bolstered by
a weekly contribution of
$50 from virtually all CEP
pulp and paper workers in
Western Canada. This effort,
later employed in the Abitibi
strike in the East,
demonstrated CEP's ability to
pull all of its resources
together throughout a mon-
umental nine-month struggle with a company
that had over a billion dollars in the bank. Even
more than all the successful community support
work, this project demonstrated just what the
new union was able to do when the need arose.

Fletcher Challenge tried to counter this display

of solidarity with threats of what the union
labelled as "international scabbing." Prevented
from doing any real scabbing because of the
strong picket lines, the company claimed that it
would turn its back on British Columbia and let its
mills there rust while it supplied its U.S. customers from the Philippines. In Campbell River a
thousand people responded by taking
to the streets carrying Canadian flags. They
suggested that the New
Zealand company get
out of town and leave them
alone to run their own affairs.

The strike could easily have
gone on longer than nine
months. It only ended when
59.3 per cent of the members
voted to accept a compromise
offer. Clearly, a lot of people were so angry with
the company that they were ready to keep up the
fight. In exchange for a limited version of what
employers like to call "flexibility" (shorthand for
more management control), the workers gained
pay increases and improved contract language ▶

> "We were fighting to retain control
> over our work," said Greg Derouin.
> . . . "We didn't just sit back as we
> might have done in the past and
> wait for the industry pressure to
> force us back to the table."

THE LYING KING

◄ *Randy Mellanby, Local 1123, stands with his union brothers and sisters against Fletcher Challenge.*

"We're still standing, and they're not here anymore," Greg Derouin said four years later, adding that the strike was "far easier" with CEP than it would have been pre-merger. Greg also believed that the strike cemented relations between pulp and paper workers in British Columbia and Eastern Canada. In the former Canadian Paperworkers Union the regions had been more separate, he said. Now, when activists from Crofton and Trois-Rivières find themselves at a convention in Toronto they seek each other out to discuss issues that concern them all. It has become a habit.

"That's the strength of the CEP right there," Greg noted. "We call each other brothers and sisters but sometimes we forget what that means. It's easier to build relations at times of adversity, but we're trying to build ourselves into a stronger union. And that's happening not just when we're on strike. We've become more of a family, and that doesn't exist in a lot of unions." △

that offered them even better protection against contracting out. The employer had gone into negotiations demanding more contracting out, so even though the mills would henceforth be operating 365 days a year, the settlement represented a clear win. True to its shorter working-hours agenda, CEP also secured a task force on job creation and shorter hours.

Other, less obvious, benefits flowed from the strike. Employers once again received the message that this new union was not to be trifled with. It would not hesitate to take on a global corporation flush with cash and determined to cut the legs out from under workers' on-the-job strength. Fletcher Challenge lost well over a billion dollars in revenue. Within a year the battered company did get out of town, and out of British Columbia. Bosses took note.

The strike could easily have gone on longer than nine months. It only ended when 59.3 per cent of the members voted to accept a compromise offer. Clearly, a lot of people were so angry with the company that they were ready to keep up the fight.

Energy and Paperworkers Union is working to manage the problem."

That same month one interest group had found another way of dealing with climate change. U.S. physicist Robert Watson, head of the Intergovernmental Panel on Climate Change and a respected scientist supported by many European governments, was removed from his position. This happened, reported London's *Financial Times*, because of "pressure from the US government and Exxon."

The Bush administration had already rejected Kyoto. Exxon-Mobil had spent over $1.5 billion financing the Climate Change Convention, an industry group opposed to action against global warming. By joining the citizens worried that the planet was under threat and coming down foursquare to urge Canada to live up to its commitment to honour the accord, CEP had shown clearly where it stood.

But its grassroots policy-making process wasn't simply producing an energy policy designed to line up against George W. Bush and his cronies in Big Oil, while siding with a global citizens' movement determined to help save the planet. CEP was in the process of developing a detailed policy plan. The transition to a green future meant fashioning a made-in-Canada energy policy – with a just transition that would boost the job-creation potential not only in the renewable energy sector but also in the entire manufacturing sector. It was a bold, carefully considered bit of union policy work that put the needs of

"This is the kind of leadership and forward thinking we need," said David Suzuki.

◄ Summer heat waves and violent storms, shrinking Great Lakes and growing forest fires, a melting polar ice cap and the flooding of entire populations are more than enough cause for Canada to rethink its approach to energy. In 1997 CEP donated to the Canadian Red Cross's Manitoba Flood Appeal.

The corporate energy agenda centres on exports to the United States. Free-trade policies have foolishly locked Canada into supplying energy-hungry but resource-starved U.S. cities and industries. Administrative vice-president Don MacNeil addresses an Alberta Federation of Labour rally in support of Petro-Can strikers.

Canadians ahead of a corporate energy agenda based on privatization, deregulation, and greed.

The new CEP policy noted that intense summer heat waves and violent winter storms, shrinking Great Lakes and growing forest fires, a melting polar ice cap and the flooding of entire populations were more than enough cause for Canada to completely rethink its approach to energy. "Climate change is real, and it is happening. It is time to act." The policy argued that the reckless exploitation of the country's forests was matched in the areas of oil, gas, coal, and electricity. "Like most of Canada's natural resource industries, the energy sector has been built on the assumption that our resources are infinite and can be drilled, mined, burned, dammed and exported without considering conservation or our own needs for long-term development."

The key words here are export, conservation, and long-term development. The corporate energy agenda centres on exports to the United States. Free-trade policies have foolishly locked Canada into supplying energy-hungry but resource-starved U.S. cities and industries, forbidding Canadians from setting their own prices for their own resources.

Natural gas, the cornerstone of numerous industries and utilities, is a case in point. CEP members work in both natural gas distribution and in the petrochemical business, where gas is the main "feedstock." They read meters, dig trenches in streets, and invoice customers. They operate and maintain plastics plants. Although the petrochemical industry uses just 10 per cent of Canada's gas, it supports 24,000 jobs, which is over 40 per cent more employment than the natural gas distribution network provides. That's because the further "downstream" gas goes, the more jobs are created. Needless to say, when gas is exported to the United States, it creates no downstream jobs. What's more, the North American Free Trade Agreement (NAFTA) makes it difficult for Canada to use its resources creatively, to generate jobs and a cleaner environment here.

Should Sable Island gas be used in Atlantic Canada to reduce reliance on dirty, coal-fired electricity? Should it be made available to Quebec's petrochemical sector? Or should it simply be sent south? The answer is obvious, but free-trade logic means that Boston's air conditioners have just as much right to Nova Scotia energy as Montreal's refineries, and there is little that public regulators in Canada can do about it. As CEP noted, "NAFTA went further than any previous trade agreement in entrenching the control of one country over the energy resources of another."

In 2002, following its successful court challenge of Ontario's hydro privatization, CEP intervened at the National Energy Board hearings on Sable Island gas exports, supporting New Brunswick's challenge to the continentalist export regime as well as arguing for "Canada First" for offshore gas.

The union also pointed out that in 2000 Quebec reacted to the electricity deregulation that had caused so much grief in the United States (Enron was a leading advocate and player) and Alberta (power prices rose by 400 per cent that year) by passing a law creating a "heritage pool" of electricity. Even though the government reserved sufficient low-cost power for Quebecers, its move has not led to NAFTA challenges; rather, it highlights the importance of government regulation to protect consumers. Mexico avoided the mess completely by exempting itself from NAFTA's energy continentalism during the treaty negotiations. Unlike Canada, Mexico did not hand the United States full access to its energy resources.

CEP rejected the entire let-the-market-decide ethos that underpins what has passed for Ottawa's energy policy – and so much of its other economic strategizing. "We must regain our sovereignty over energy pricing," said the 2002 policy. Without such control, Canadians forfeit the ability not only to set

In a northern climate, energy is too important to be left to the whims of the market and the multinationals that control it. Allowing this to happen is akin to treating us all like a set of gas pumps the day before a long weekend.

their own energy prices but also to shape a jobs-oriented economic strategy based on their own natural resources. Ceding power to the U.S. government and corporations makes it difficult to conserve those non-renewable resources.

The essence of the policy developed by the CEP at the height of the debate over the Kyoto accord was that energy is not just another commodity. In a northern climate, energy is too important to be left to the whims of the market and the multinationals that control it. Allowing this to happen is akin to treating us all like a set of gas pumps the day before a long weekend.

As the union put it, decisions over energy "should not be left to the so-called 'free market' with its fundamental drive for short-term profit regardless of social cost, environmental impact or consequences for worker health and safety. The Enron bankruptcy of 2001 demonstrated the folly of allowing the corporate equivalent of Mississippi riverboat gamblers to run an essential service as critical as energy supply."

CHAPTER EIGHT

A few days in May, Part 2: REGINA

I LEFT FORT MCMURRAY on an early flight to Edmonton and Calgary, where I had a long wait before I could depart for Regina. I had lots of time to catch up on the news of the day – or yesterday, May Day, celebrated by the Catholic Church as the Feast of St. Joseph the Worker, by trade unionists as International Workers Day, and by others simply as a rite of spring.

I knew that Edmonton had a May Day march and celebration to mark the start of its union-oriented May Week Labour Arts Festival because I'd heard an interview with one of the organizers on CBC Radio. The *Edmonton Journal*'s May Day coverage consisted of a wire report cobbled together from various correspondents. There had been big demonstrations in London, England, as well as in Sydney, Berlin, Singapore, and Athens. The lead paragraphs described a "rampage" by "masked anarchist youths" in Berlin. In London they burned an effigy of George W. Bush. The *Journal* did not bother with the peaceful local event at home in Edmonton.

Journalists are supposed to be cynical and see themselves as worldly, so I suppose I shouldn't have been surprised. But I could still only shake my head. I turned to a special supplement, jointly published by the *Journal* and *Calgary Herald*, on Fort McMurray. The editors had sent five reporters to the town I had

▲ *It's not all about how to deal with tear gas, the police, and the media. The sessions included labour history and civil disobedience. CEP members attend the "Building a Culture of Resistance" course.*

> What I found most startling was that the one and only mention of unions consisted of the owner of a small plumbing and heating business blaming, among other things, "heavy union involvement" for his decision to close up shop.

just visited. They came up with twenty-one stories filling an ad-packed sixteen pages. I got lots of statistics and quotes from businessmen, politicians, and a few community agency people. I learned that the big oil companies were "partners in philanthropy," that the Syncrude president was a rare oil patch executive because he lived in town, and that Aboriginal workers were "efficient" and "productive."

There was news that companies involved in the expansion boom were blaming staggering cost overruns (one project had gone from $1 billion to $3.5 billion) on high labour costs and the low dollar. There was no reference to the possibility of any mismanagement – which was not surprising, given the business-friendly coverage. But what I found most startling was that the one and only mention of unions consisted of the owner of a small plumbing and heating business blaming, among other things, "heavy union involvement" for his decision to close up shop. There was, however, a colour photo of the U.S. energy secretary.

Media bias is no surprise, and the recent wave of corporate concentration hadn't helped at all. But this sort of puffery brought it all home because of the short time I had just spent in Fort McMurray learning about what CEP had been doing to support community activities. Airbrushing this sort of work from the record seemed somehow worse than the usual attacks on unions as selfish oversized organizations run by "bosses," interested only in looking out for Number One.

When I got to Calgary's busy airport, I picked up a copy of that city's daily. (I admit to being a newspaper junky.) Scanning the *Herald*, I noticed one of the national editorials that Southam papers were now being forced to carry under their new ownership – the previous owner, Conrad Black, had fled from Canada and passed the papers to Winnipeg's Asper family and its CanWest Global Communications Corp. Papers across the country would be carrying CanWest Global predictions that the upcoming G8 summit in Kananaskis would surely be met by the same "thuggery" that had apparently just unfolded around the world yesterday "as a result of that outdated left-wing shibboleth, May Day 'celebrations.'" The focus of the editorial was a union-sponsored seminar in Calgary called "Building a Culture of Resistance."

It was no surprise that the Asper interests denounced citizens concerned about poverty and environmental degradation as violent troublemakers determined to disrupt yet another gathering of "democracy's leaders." What was more interesting was the editorial's tone, similar to that employed a few months earlier by senior executive David Asper, who got mad when journalists withdrew their bylines to protest the introduction of national editorials. Asper attacked his own employees as "riff-raff" bent on "childish protest." Rather than addressing the arguments of the globalization critics, Southam's wacky editorial mocked protestors for eating organic food and playing Hacky Sack. Their colourful puppets and costumes were a "camouflage for violence" that would result in "lost business." The editorial specifically targeted unions for backing the movement against corporate globalization. After the inevitable anti-globalization violence at the upcoming G8 summit, "the usual organizations and labour unions" would complain about police brutality.

In Regina I picked up the *Leader-Post* and, sure enough, there was the same message. After arriving at the CEP office I found out a bit about what that Calgary discussion of building a culture of resistance had been all about.

It turned out that CEP rep David Durning had been one of the main organizers of the event. It also turned out that the G8 preparatory meeting had not been a seminar on rock-throwing after all. Rather, the emphasis had been on building local opposition to globalization as well as preparing for the upcoming protests that would confront Democracy's Leaders. That's because, however high-profile the summits and the protests have become, the decisions taken behind the barbed wire were being enforced in factories and offices and streets and police stations around the world.

Indeed, David's educational materials – part of the CEP "Tools for Trouble-makers" course kit – emphasized organizing democratic meetings by recognizing difference and developing respect across class, race, and gender lines. It

Rather than addressing the arguments of the globalization critics, Southam's wacky editorial mocked protestors for eating organic food and playing Hacky Sack.

wasn't all about how to deal with tear gas, the police, and the media. The sessions included labour history and civil disobedience.

David Durning is a veteran organizer born not far from Westray and the other widowmaker mines of Nova Scotia's Pictou County. He services CEP locals representing hotel, paper, chemical, and television workers and feels that the way you communicate with people is as important as anything else. His "Tools for Troublemakers" material reminded "white guys" that they tend to bond with each other, creating an internal organizing culture that's alienating to others. "Be aware of how often you ask people to do something as opposed to asking other people 'What needs to be done?'" This sort of advice, together with the reminder that it is the responsibility of leaders to develop more leaders, reminded me of just how different the growing movement for international solidarity was from the caricatures retailed by the corporate media.

Another message we get from the Aspers and Blacks of the world is that public control of just about anything is a Bad Thing. After being in Alberta – where you get the feeling that they'd privatize the sidewalks if they could figure out a way to charge tolls – I wanted to get a sense of where things stood at SaskTel, North America's last publicly controlled phone company of any size.

> "Be aware of how often you ask people to do something as opposed to asking other people 'What needs to be done?'"
>
> • DAVID DURNING

SaskTel and the "Public Interest" campaign

THE WORKERS AT SASKTEL have been organized since 1944, well before the founding of the Communications Workers of Canada (CWC), one of the CEP's founding unions. Unlike unions in Alberta, where workers have always had an uphill fight against anti-union governments, in Saskatchewan, under a succession of CCF and NDP governments, labour has often had the advantage of a level playing field. What was it like, I wondered, for CEP members at SaskTel in this public-enterprise-friendly place?

Saskatchewan is a small, agricultural province struggling with drought. Like workers in the softwood lumber industry, its farmers face a crisis stoked by the protectionism of a free-trade government in the United States. Although the NDP government remained committed to maintaining public control of its telephone company, CEP had launched "In the Public Interest," a campaign to defend SaskTel against the let-the-market-decide zealots of the Saskatchewan Party, the latest incarnation of the Tories.

"Would a company like Bell provide decent service to small-town Saskatchewan?" asked Rhoda Cossar, a former operator and former president of CEP Local 1S. "Rural Saskatchewan is already struggling as it is."

Rhoda, who now works as a CEP rep servicing several locals, including

◀ A public phone company emphasizes good service to everyone, not just big business and big-city customers. A SaskTel sales clerk serves a customer at the North Telmart store.

the SaskTel locals, told me about the advantages of having a public phone company. SaskTel emphasizes good service to everyone, not just big business and big-city customers. What's more, it pumps millions of dollars of profits back into the public treasury: $783 million between 1987 and 2001. At the same time it has not been content with POTS, plain ordinary telephone service. It competes effectively in wireless, digital interactive video and even security services, all of which provokes howls of outrage from the Saskatchewan Party. That party's members maintain that public companies have no business in business.

The CEP's "In the Public Interest" campaign is a pre-emptive strike against the privatizers. It points out that SaskTel provides good jobs in communities where good jobs are becoming an endangered species. It is the people of Saskatchewan who make the investment decisions and decide how the corporation's profits are to be distributed, not out-of-province shareholders. The decisions and the money stay in Saskatchewan. From the worker's point of view, it's always good to be able to wield as much influence with your employer as, say, its bankers have. If she needs to deal with an important problem, Rhoda Cossar knows she can always pick up the phone and talk to the president of SaskTel.

If this sounds utopian, it's only because we live in a time when a "public" company has come to mean an enterprise with shares publicly traded on the stock market, not a concern owned by the public as a whole. Against this background a company like SaskTel stands out. Unlike Bell, it does not treat its employees like disposable diapers – use and throw away.

Although the NDP government remained committed to maintaining public control of its telephone company, CEP had launched "In the Public Interest," a campaign to defend SaskTel against the let-the-market-decide zealots of the Saskatchewan Party, the latest incarnation of the Tories.

Still, as I learned when Rhoda Cossar and I sat down with a group of Local 1S members, life at SaskTel is not some sort of worker paradise. We gathered around a table in a former Jehovah's Witnesses church near the Regina airport. Volunteer labour had transformed the neat-as-a-pin building into a union office. As with the Fort McMurray food bank, having skilled trades workers comes in handy. I started off with a standard question: "Why did you decide to get involved in the trade union movement?"

Connie Buchan had a quick, simple answer. She wanted a say in her working life and when she started out at SaskTel scheduling was too strict, production was everything. "The management style was dictatorial and I wanted to change that," she said.

Like the CEP people in Fort McMurray – and most everywhere else I visited – Connie was forty-something and had spent more than her share of hours sitting around tables like this one, thrashing out contract language, grievances, and internal union politics. She explained that even though the NDP may be committed to the public sector, it had not taken her long to figure out that handling calls at SaskTel was not really all that much different from setting up a lathe in a paper mill's machine shop or making up pages at a big-city newspaper. A boss is a boss is a boss.

"People assumed that because you were a government worker there was no abuse and everything was wonderful," she said. But as her union got stronger, things improved. Local 1S succeeded in balancing management rights with worker rights.

"People assumed that because you were a government worker there was no abuse and everything was wonderful." Wrong. CEP workers at SaskTel had to strike in 1996

D. DURNING

104

Still, as phone companies in neighbouring Manitoba and Alberta were privatized and management noticed what was happening at places like Bell, there was a spillover effect in Saskatchewan. Along with deregulation, it all added up to the usual employer talk about being leaner and more flexible. "We're doing more now with fewer people and fewer resources," said Connie.

One of her colleagues who works as a technician agreed. He described more measurement and monitoring as the employer put the pressure on people to produce what it had decided the average worker should produce. He mentioned that SaskTel had put electronic monitors in service vehicles so that the employer would be able to plot the movements and activities of the repair workers. Connie reminded her male colleagues that the women who worked as operators at SaskTel had been going through this sort of thing for years.

This sort of debate – between men and women, between workers who do different jobs – is not unfamiliar to union activists, and it's not just confined to the telecommunications companies. It is woven into the fabric of working life. The same kind of tension came up again when our discussion turned to how things had unfolded since Local 1S, along with the rest of the Communications and Electrical Workers of Canada, decided to merge with the energy and paper unions to form CEP.

There was general agreement that it's better to be big than small these days. What with employers saying we need to do more with less in the workplace and we need more business and less government in society at large, Local 1S needed a more muscular outfit like the CEP.

But even as she stressed the ability of the merged union to put its weight behind the defence of medicare, Connie brought up something that Rhoda Cossar had told me about earlier. Some people at SaskTel feel like they are now smaller fish in a bigger pond – that the service they get from CEP does not measure up to what was available when they had a rep all to themselves. The problem is partly about money, partly about identity.

"You can't just put three families in one house and expect everyone to get along and not want to do things their own way," Connie said. "There's no way you can make people forget where they came from. We have to honour that and respect it and build it into our structure at the CEP. We're not doing that."

Growing pains and mixed feelings

THE GROWING PAINS of a ten-year-old union are not that different from the experience of anyone approaching teenage years. Life does not always seem easy. It takes work to balance the needs of locals big and small, to service the old and organize the new while staying nimble enough to respond effectively

> The growing pains of a ten-year-old union are not that different from the experience of anyone approaching teenage years.

Nastasha Goudar wondered just what kind of lessons Regina school-children were learning in a program called "McBooks" that offered free french fries to kids who were reading enough.

to the latest employer offensive. It is not surprising that activists like Connie have mixed feelings about the merged union. "When we do campaigns like the one around the G8 summit in Kananaskis and with our involvement in the larger labour movement, I think we do better than we ever did with the CWC. But validating our own locals and giving them what they need – I don't think we're doing that good a job."

Another participant in our discussion had a slightly different view of things. Cam Britton said he had not been very involved in the union before the merger. Since then he has become secretary-treasurer of Local 1S. For him, it's understandable that people with longer histories in the union have the feelings they do. "I come in and hear about all these sectors. I don't have that background."

Cam had found that the CEP experience broadened the way he saw the world around him. "You really learn a lot about the other industries. There's brothers and sisters in the paper sector who are facing this softwood lumber dispute. Years ago I would have thought, 'Gee, that's kind of a ripoff.' But now I'm mad."

The next day I accompanied Dave Durning to a teach-in he helped to organize along with the Council of Canadians and the Saskatchewan Federation of Labour. They held "Globalization 101" in a municipally owned community building where you could rent a clean, bright room for twenty dollars. A chess club was busy upstairs, and in the big room on the main floor some forty people had given up a sunny springtime Saturday to learn about how global corporations were downsizing democracy. At the front of the room someone had draped a banner that said "Organize/Syndiquer."

I was struck by how the teach-in was hosted by young women under thirty, community activists who were already veterans of the movement. They put on a skit and used a word that hadn't been employed during my discussions with the CEP activists: "awesome." There were the usual formal presentations, workshops, and breakout groups. I noticed that in his presentation about the G8 and jobs, Dave didn't come across as any sort of slick expert, even though he was equipped with a Power Point presentation he had spent half a day preparing. It was only a forty-minute session. A veteran union educator, he let others do most of the talking. At a session on globalization and youth, Natasha Goudar wondered just what kind of lessons Regina schoolchildren were learning in a program called "McBooks" that offered free french fries to kids who were reading enough.

Crappy jobs. Higher tuition. More student debt. Unequal distribution of wealth. "As young people," Nastasha said, "we have so much longer to live with all of this."

K. NEWMAN

◄ *A publicly owned company like SaskTel stands out. Unlike Bell, it does not treat its employees like disposable diapers – use and throw away.*

I came away from Fort McMurray, Regina, and Globalization 101 with mixed feelings. It had been sobering to hear a Vancouver activist tell the teach-in that twenty thousand people had showed up for the opening of an IKEA outlet. Apparently the B.C. labour movement had spent big money and a lot of effort to organize a demonstration of that many people against the wrecking crew now in office in Victoria. But at the same time, I felt hopeful, buoyed up by the energy of Keith and Rollie, Rhoda, Connie, Cam, and Natasha. I recalled Dave Durning's reaction when I asked him how many hours he put in every week. "Oh, maybe seventy . . . maybe."

I had the impression that he was low-balling it. "Isn't CEP the shorter-hours union?"

He only smiled.

CHAPTER NINE

Shorter hours:
"WE ARE ON STRIKE FOR FAMILY VALUES"

A SNOWMAN STOOD beside the Loyalist Parkway holding a CEP picket sign: "Just Say No to Mandatory Overtime."

Local 2190 was on strike against the Canadian arm of Lafarge, the world's biggest cement company. The huge grey plant near Kingston, Ont., is just west of the historic village of Bath, where United Empire Loyalist settlers landed during the American Revolution. The rocky land wasn't that great for farming, but the limestone and waterfront location made it an ideal site for a cement plant. There was a giant quarry behind the Lafarge plant. The CEP snowman stared out at the icy waters where Lake Ontario turns into the St. Lawrence River.

The strike started on December 4, 2001, and every day and evening that winter the little knot of men walked around in the slush or cold. Bundled up in snowmobile suits and hunting garb, they leaned into a wind that whipped off the water, which didn't freeze that winter. It did get icy enough to give new meaning to the notion of wind chill.

▲ *"People with twenty-five years told me during the strike they had never seen the local so strong. And that's the way we went back."*

• DOUG CHISHOLM,
PRESIDENT,
LOCAL 2190

"People think unions only go on strike for more money. We're out here, in a peculiar way, for less money."

It was shift work, a constant to-and-fro on the tarmac, twelve hours of picket duty every few days. For the strike they would arrive in pickups before dawn and leave after dark. A notice pinned up at the post office in Bath paid off, as supporters kept arriving with loads of firewood. By early March the burn barrel had consumed ten cords of wood. Tending the fire became a welcome task.

"You like poking things into holes, don't you?" someone said with a laugh as a striker bent down to stoke the fire, jamming a branch into one of the jagged holes in the bottom of the rusting barrel. Some thirty metres further up the pavement stone-faced security guards, rent-a-cops, stayed warm in their purple vans, motors idling. A battered wire lawn chair blocked the road, separating the two groups. The main background noise came from behind the guards – a ceaseless dull roar from the ball mill where the limestone was still being crushed, despite the best efforts of the striking cement workers. They were on strike for less pay.

"Lafarge is showing contempt for these workers and their families with its outrageous demands," CEP president Brian Payne said when he joined the pickets soon after the strike started. "Its disregard for the workers' legitimate health and safety concerns caused by excessive hours is simply archaic."

The sixty-four members of Local 2190 would occupy the forlorn piece of pavement well into the summer of 2002. Strikes are usually about wages and benefits. This one was about time – about whether people still have a right to control when – and how long – they work. "We're currently working fourteen months a year, and that doesn't seem to be enough for them," said Doug Chisholm, a maintenance apprentice with fifteen years' seniority. There was so much overtime that he figured he had already put in eighteen years at Lafarge. "People think unions only go on strike for more money. We're out here, in a peculiar way, for less money."

Lafarge is one of the larger employers in this area west of Kingston, and during Doug's years at the plant its production has gone up. But at the same time its workforce has been cut in half, from 112 workers to 63. When the strike started the company wanted even more overtime, demanding the removal of contract language that allowed CEP members to refuse overtime if they had a legitimate reason. For the already stressed workers, a legitimate reason could be having to be home for their children. Lafarge wanted the workers to be on call all day every day. Its proposed contract language would only allow workers to refuse overtime if they had already worked sixteen hours that day. It also wanted them to carry beepers so that they could always be on call.

Lafarge management had also tended to neglect basic maintenance. When equipment that has been allowed to deteriorate finally breaks down, there's an emergency that requires overtime. It's not the most pleasant place to work, especially on scorching hot summer days when you have to crawl around among the bird shit and the rotting pigeon carcasses at the top of a seven-storey feed end trying to replace a burnt-out bearing that the boss had ignored despite warnings from the workers.

Management had promoted a culture of longer hours at the plant. Doug should know. His father worked there for thirty-one years and Doug himself has been part of the aging workforce (two-thirds of the workers have enough seniority to retire in seven years) long enough to see the corrosive pattern.

"Time and time again you hear from these senior employees that they missed their kids growing up," Doug said as a small knot of pickets huddled against the wind. "The next thing you know you turn around and your kids are eighteen years old and they're moving out of the house. Every hour of overtime you work takes away from your family."

"The people who decide how much we work aren't the ones doing the work," added Dan White, an apprentice with sixteen years at Lafarge. White spends part of what spare time he has taking courses towards his millwright ticket. He is separated from his wife and values the time he gets to spend with his young son. He resents it when the boss tells him at the last minute that, no, he won't be able to be with the boy that day as he had planned. He has to work overtime. Again.

"I'm at a time of life that I want to slow down," said White, forty-six. "I've got a life outside Lafarge."

Getting a life outside work is what this landmark strike was all about. It was also about an issue as old as the labour movement itself. If longer hours are part of the culture that Lafarge management was trying to promote, the union that challenged them was going in the opposite direction.

CEP has deep roots in the struggle for shorter hours. The printers and typographers who were among the first Canadian workers ever to organize were forerunners of today's CEP media component. In 1827 printers formed the Société Typographique du Québec. Five years later printers in York (now Toronto) formed what would become the Toronto Typographical Union, which took a vanguard role in the fight for the fifty-four-hour week. In 1872 the TTU faced down scabs during its successful strike for shorter hours. That year witnessed an upsurge of labour agitation for the nine-hour day, and Ottawa passed one of the first-ever laws legitimizing unions.

At a Hamilton demonstration in 1872 a machinist used a horse-drawn cart to display a gravestone with the epitaph "Died 15th of May, the ten hour system." It was all part of a historic wave of strikes prompted by a surge in

▲ *The Toronto Typographical Union (TTU) took a vanguard role in the fight for the fifty-four-hour week. The TTU is today CEP Local 910. The president, James Kilpatrick, speaks to the 1994 CEP convention, dressed as a printer circa 1870.*

MURRAY MOSHER

The spillover effect: "Thank God it's Thursday"

NOWHERE ELSE DOES CEP'S role as the Shorter Hours Union mesh more with its growing reputation as a community-oriented union than in Sarnia, Ont. Here they say "Thank God it's Thursday." That's because back in 1973 a CEP predecessor union moved to a thirty-seven and a third workweek at Polysar, now Bayer Rubber.

Since that time, five other CEP plants in town have begun to take "Happy Fridays." Every third Friday is a day off. Cathy Cichonski, deputy chief steward of CEP Local 914, explained it in the simplest possible terms: "Today is Happy Friday because we're not at work."

People have different ways of spending their extra free time, but one thing unites much of the community — an awareness that it is an idea whose time has come. Cathy spends her Happy Fridays either at home alone enjoying quiet time when her children aren't around or volunteering at their school. "My kids like it when I can help out at school or go on class trips. Happy Fridays put a lot back into the community."

Although she has always had Happy Fridays since she started at Bayer twenty-one years ago, Cathy knows that others in town have only recently made the gain.

The plan has become infectious. As she relaxed in the lounge of the big CEP union hall on a Friday afternoon, Darcie Tripp described how the gains achieved by the union in the chemical industry had changed workers' lives throughout the community. Darcie is a medical secretary at the Sarnia General Hospital, where she is vice-president of the Office and Professional Employees International Union. The workers there just got their Happy Fridays in the last round of bargaining.

"It's a spillover from the chemical valley industry workers," she said. "Everything is pattern bargaining. Whether you work in health care or in industry, you always know what everybody else gets in their collective agreement. I love them. A three-day weekend. Perfect!"

> **People have different ways of spending their extra free time, but one thing unites much of the community – an awareness that it is an idea whose time has come.**

Sarnia, Ont., birthplace of Happy Fridays. CEP workers have been enjoying shorter hours here for some thirty years. ▶

G. HILL PHOTO INC

industrialization and productivity in Canada, Britain, and the United States. Fighting for shorter hours was a way for workers to get their share of the new wealth. As one U.S. labour reformer of the day explained, "Men who are compelled to sell their labour, very naturally desire to sell the smallest portion of their time for the largest possible price. They are merchants of their time. It is their only available capital."

The Lafarge strikers on the Loyalist Parkway were carrying on the tradition. In the 1830s, when Kingston-area workers demanded shorter hours, the Loyalist press denounced their ideas about "Atheism, Republicanism and Revolution," labelling them "pernicious."

By 2001 bosses had refined their rhetoric somewhat. Just before the strike, Lafarge managers gave one of their pep talks. CEP members call them "Atta Boy!" sessions. They heard that they were second in low-cost production among the Lafarge plants in the Great Lakes region. Rather than starting a ritual chant of "We're Number Two," the workers walked out. They wanted the company to forget about its beeper plans and instead create more jobs so that

The idea of working shorter hours is so entrenched in Sarnia that CEP negotiators at Bayer proposed reducing the workweek to thirty-six hours when the plant faced the possibility of layoffs in 1994. Although management rejected the idea in favour of establishing special work crews to avoid job losses, the CEP bargaining committee was convinced that the membership was going to support the idea despite the loss in pay. Indeed, three-quarters of the members voted to back the proposal.

Even the supervisors at the rubber plant caught the shorter hours bug. When management decided to take the Happy Fridays away from the supervisors in order to save money, the front-line management immediately approached CEP and asked to join up. The company retreated even before the cards could be produced. △

◄ *A laboratory technician at Bayer Rubber, Sarnia. In 1973 the ECWU moved to a thirty-seven and a third week at Polysar, now Bayer Rubber. Since then, five other CEP plants in town have begun to take Happy Fridays.*

G. HILL PHOTO INC

The 1997 study "More Jobs, More Fun" confirmed that, like heroin and potato chips, shorter hours are addictive.

they would not have to work so much overtime. It didn't matter to them that the change would mean less money.

Just as the strike started, the cement colossus was finishing what it boasted was an all-time high in fourth-quarter profits. The French multinational, the biggest producer of building materials in the world, reported that shipments from Bath and its other Ontario and Quebec operations were the key to boosting Canadian cement output.

Work at a cement plant is cold in winter, hot in summer, dusty all year round. When the employer is boosting production while cutting the workforce, there is also lots of on-the-job pressure. But Lafarge's job-reduction agenda produced not only a heavy burden of overtime. It also generated what the bosses called the "self-directed workforce." They eliminated all front-line supervisors and gave some workers business cards, calling them "team leaders" and persuading them to help organize things. (There was no mention of the workers deciding on overtime levels.) Going into the strike, the workers had mixed feelings about a scheme that meant union members would take orders from other union members. Early in the strike Doug Chisholm described this version of a team concept as "touchy." It was safe to say that by the end of the strike Lafarge might experience a bit more difficulty in its efforts to persuade the workers that they were all on the same big team.

The pickets beside the burn barrel had personal experience confirming the findings of the landmark CEP shorter hours study, "More Jobs, More Fun." They knew that the long overtime hours they worked could be replaced by full-time jobs, that employers were generally opposed to shorter hours but that workers were willing to consider working less, especially if it meant that someone who needed a job could get one. Most of them had put in enough years at the lakeside cement plant that their union wages enabled them to buy boats and summertime cottages. Instead of spending all that extra time in the heat and dust, they'd just as soon take it easy.

Lead electrician Jurriaan Vandenberg had eighteen years at Lafarge. He didn't think it was unreasonable to have workers on call. "That's fine, *if* you've got lots of people to cover the work," said Vandenberg, who said he put in five to six hundred hours of overtime a year. "The union is just saying 'Fair's fair.' You've got to have enough people to do the work, but they don't want to hire."

For Vandenberg, money isn't an issue. His wife works as a nurse at Kingston General. But life is hectic because of all the shift work and overtime. Nights are always a problem. "Luckily our oldest can babysit now, but with ball and hockey and dancing, life is still a real juggling act."

The Lafarge workers ▶ *struck for less pay. They wanted the world's biggest cement company to create more jobs so that they wouldn't have to work overtime that sometimes added up to an extra two months a year. At first the company refused. After seven months facing the CEP picket line, it changed its mind.*

The shorter hours union

IN ITS TEN SHORT YEARS CEP has become known as the Shorter Hours Union. In her study "Working Less for More Jobs," CEP researcher Julie White revealed that downsizing by B.C. pulp and paper companies had reduced the workforce so that there were not enough workers to cover negotiated time off. What's more, the study found out that even though companies would actually save money by hiring more people and cutting overtime, managers caught up in the downsizing frenzy still believed that having less people meant that they would make more money. Some 73 per cent of CEP members in the B.C. mills were willing to reduce overtime to create jobs.

The union had already proved that working shorter hours was working for CEP members right across the country. In Sarnia they had had their "Happy Fridays" since 1973. SaskTel workers in Saskatchewan got twenty-six extra holidays each by taking every second Friday off. The 1997 study "More Jobs, More Fun" confirmed what everyone who had tried working less already knew. Like heroin and potato chips, shorter hours are addictive. Once you start, it's hard to stop. If management tried to return to longer hours, the withdrawal symptoms among the workers would be severe: "They'd walk en masse and I think we'd probably be out there until hell froze over ..."

A worker at the Belgo mill in Shawinigan explained the issue in a way that the Lafarge workers clearly understood. Years of gains by their union had given both the pulp and paper workers and the cement workers good wages. For the Shawinigan worker, anyone addicted to overtime had it wrong: "By the end of the year they have earned more money than we have, but they pay more in taxes too.

If management tried to return to longer hours, the withdrawal symptoms among the workers would be severe: "They'd walk en masse and I think we'd probably be out there until hell froze over ..."

115

They are going to have more TV sets or telephones or whatever. More money does not necessarily increase your quality of life. You consume more ..."

A year after CEP had completed its study of working less for more jobs, the Shorter Hours Union was ready to strengthen its commitment to reducing working hours. At its 2000 convention the union passed resolution G-12 on hours of work. The delegates did not agree that shorter hours would necessarily be negotiated with no loss in pay. For CEP, shorter hours are

EEL RIVER, N.B.

"They'd kill us if we ever went off the shorter hours"

ALDEO DOUCET LIVES in Northern New Brunswick, where the unemployment rate hovers around 22 per cent – in a good year. He and his wife Bridget were expecting their first child in 1988 when he got a job at the Canadian Pacific Forest Products mill in Dalhousie. The hiring was the direct result of a deal negotiated by Local 263, making Dalhousie the only plant in the Atlantic region on shorter hours.

Cutting the deal was not easy, said Sandy Beckingham, a papermaker and long-time activist at the mill in nearby Dalhousie. It was not only a matter of persuading management. The membership was divided on the "6/3" proposal – eight-hour shifts with six days' work and three days off. Indeed, feelings were running so high that when one worker who had been actively pushing the new shorter work time

> "We have more time with the kids, more time to do things," Aldeo said. "Before, I never went to the gym. I was tired all the time. Now I have lots of time and energy."

schedule suddenly died, a piece of graffiti appeared on the washroom wall at the mill: "One less for the 6/3." Tires got slashed. But as so often happens, once the new hours were introduced, the controversy evaporated. In 1993 the union opted for a twelve-hour shift, with the members working four days on and five days off.

"They'd kill us if we ever went off the shorter hours," Sandy reported. He explained that as a result of the shorter workweek there were 11 per cent more people working at the mill, now owned by Bowater Paper Company. A young fellow of nineteen got hired in early 2002, along with the mill's first woman worker.

For Aldeo Doucet of Eel River, the new hours meant not only that his job was more secure, but also that he had a job. Without the reduced simply another benefit, like better pensions or better coverage in the dental plan. Sometimes, particularly in the sectors such as energy or paper where CEP represents workers with relatively high rates of pay, they are ready to trade money for time.

In 2002 Bill Saunders, a veteran CEP member whose typographical union has a long history of struggling for shorter hours, explained his understanding of how the labour movement – and especially CEP – has regarded the fight. It

D. BOUZEK

◀ *The shorter hours schedule at the Dalhousie mill gives Aldeo Doucet of Eel River, N.B., more time with his family. He is often home to prepare lunch for Caroline, twelve, and Eric, nine.*

work-time schedule, Bowater would be providing less than four hundred jobs, not the 458 that it had managed in 2002. Aldeo had been laid off for six years when the mill shut down two paper machines. He worked in a hardware store and for $10 an hour at a non-union sawmill. "It was like winning the 6/49, getting that job in the mill back." He found that the shorter hours schedule gave him more time with his family. Now he only misses supper twice a week and is often home to prepare lunch for Caroline, twelve, and Eric, nine.

"We have more time with the kids, more time to do things," Aldeo said. "Before, I never went to the gym. I had no time and I was tired all the time. Now I have lots of time and lots of energy."

He uses part of the extra time and energy to do volunteer work. Like many small communities,

Eel River depends on a volunteer fire department, and Aldeo gets called about twenty-five times a year. The fire hall down the street doubles as a social club, where the members have painstakingly refurbished a 1936 fire truck. There are thirty-three other volunteers, including the fire chief, who is also a CEP member, a millwright at Bowater.

There are, however, still outstanding issues over work time at the Dalhousie mill. Workers still take overtime, something management likes but Sandy Beckingham hates. He figures that his members are well paid and don't need the extra work that others could use. "Every time there's an overtime shift, there's one too many as far as I'm concerned." But he is still in the minority on that issue. △

is not simply something for $26-an-hour papermakers in Shawinigan. It also affects the workers struggling for union recognition at Viva Pharmaceutical in suburban Vancouver or the newly organized people at Toronto's *Korea Times*.

"Would working people like to have more leisure time? Yes or no?" asked Bill.

"It's just about quality of life. Part of quality of life is being able to earn an amount of money that allows you to live a reasonable life. That means the wages of low-wage earners have to be brought up, so that they're not forced to work more hours to earn a living. Shorter hours is a piece of that. If low wage-earners have to be brought up faster than high wage-earners, then that's what has to be done."

Strikes, scabs, and a tragic paradox

ROSE McCARTHY IS A MILLWRIGHT, one of two women among the sixty-four CEP strikers at Lafarge Canada. She started at the cement plant in 1986 and since then she has had four children. She even met her husband on the job.

"We just happened to catch each other's eye," she recalled. "Went out on a date and it was love after that."

One of the electricians had rigged a line from the Lafarge pumping station next to the pier where the lake freighters dock. He hadn't asked for employer permission. Rose and Ken were sitting in the strike trailer by the river, taking cover from a sleet storm. Ken Mowbray agreed with his wife – but only partly.

"Regardless of what she'll tell you, she asked me out," he said, with a laugh. "We hit it off pretty much immediately. Pretty much one of the best things that ever happened to me."

Their relationship must be pretty strong. Given that the punishing overtime work schedule demanded by Lafarge involves lots of evenings, nights, and weekends, it's a wonder Rose and Ken are still together. In 2000 a University of Montreal study revealed that couples with at least one partner working non-standard hours were twice as likely to split as those with more normal work schedules. The longer hours demanded by leading multinationals make it plain. Capitalism is anti-family.

"All too often today's families must live on the leftovers of human energy and time," concluded the Vanier Institute of the Family.

Rose and Ken figure it's worth being on strike to get more control over their lives. With four young children at home, they have been forced into the rat race familiar to so many parents.

"We hardly get to see our kids as it is," Rose said. "We see them at most four

The longer hours demanded by leading multinationals make it plain. Capitalism is anti-family.

and a half hours through the workweek, if you count travelling time. Weekends are full with grocery shopping and housework and homework and all the other things that go along with life. I really believe in this strike and the family values behind it. We don't have a lot of time to spend with our kids."

The Lafarge strike was long and difficult. Rather than taking the needs of workers and their families seriously by agreeing to hire more people, Lafarge brought in scabs; and nothing inflames a labour dispute like scabs. The Lafarge scabs arrived in school buses, escorted by the police. The company had the law on its side, and the CEP strikers seethed as the scabs crossed the picket line. It didn't happen often because Lafarge set up seven residential trailers behind the security guards with the little red fingerprint logos on their jackets.

Loyalist Township immediately ordered the trailers removed because the company was breaking the local zoning bylaw. The company simply refused to obey the law, confirming the old saying about laws being like spiderwebs – they let the big flies through but catch little bugs. The CEP strikers were bitter about a company that enjoyed the protection of the law to bring in scabs but just ignored the law when it came to sheltering them. The Lafarge strategy was clear. The multinational was rich enough to lead the little township on a merry chase through the courts while keeping production going.

Still, CEP had a deep well of support in the local community. It went beyond horn-honking and free firewood. Not long after the strike started Rev. Andy Chisholm (no relation to Doug Chisholm of Local 2190) of the Anglican

"A scab is a two-legged animal with a corkscrew soul, a water brain, a combination backbone of jelly and glue. Where others have hearts, he carries a tumour of rotten principles."

◀ *"We are on strike for family values." Lafarge failed to take the needs of workers and their families seriously.*

Church in Bath brought a poem to the picket line. Though the corporate press calls them "replacement workers," Jack London had a different name for them: "After God had finished the rattlesnake, the toad, and the vampire, he had some awful substance left with which he made a scab.

"A scab is a two-legged animal with a corkscrew soul, a water brain, a combination backbone of jelly and glue. Where others have hearts, he carries a tumour of rotten principles."

Despite the challenges from the company and the legal system, the Lafarge dispute had its dividends. Strikes can often galvanize local unions, bringing people together. "A lot of our guys have never been through a strike," Ken Mowbray said. "I think it is jelling the local union."

Ten weeks into the strike Rose McCarthy gave birth to Zachary McCarthy-Mowbray, who had been on the line with his mom in utero and would return

MASSON, QUEBEC

"We had a moral and social imperative to act"

IT WAS A HOT DAY in August when Paul Raby heard that the list had been posted on the bulletin board in the hall. He was on holiday, and he expected that his long years of service at the Papier Masson mill on the Ottawa River would mean that the job cuts accompanying the installation of the new thermo-mechanical pulping (TMP) process would not affect him, at least directly. He was wrong.

"I got to the hallway and I saw the list and then 'Err ...' I saw that I was fired. I was in the grey area. Let me tell you, that's quite the slap in the face after eighteen years of service."

Yves Chenier, the father of three young children, arrived at the same time and got the same news. His reaction was the same –

"devastating, you're in a state of shock" – but he recalled being hopeful at the same time. "We still knew that we had a strong executive that could negotiate something."

As it turned out, the executive of CEP Local 11 lived up to Yves's hopes. In fact, the local at Papier Masson had been working towards shorter hours for a number of years. It was one of the most modern newsprint mills in the Canadian paper industry even before the introduction of TMP. Local 11 president Richard Lahaie was proud of the high-speed Beloit paper machine named "La Lièvre" for the river on which the lumberjacks once drove logs to the mill. The mill no longer used roundwood, Richard explained, and the new TMP process meant that the whole mill was running at full speed with as an infant. What kind of job will Zachary find when he grows up? Will there be fewer hours because new unions like CEP have successfully continued the old labour tradition of pushing for shorter hours? Why shorter hours, anyway?

Human beings have the ways and means of producing enough for everyone on the planet. Some of us have more than enough. Indeed, one of the world's problems is curbing the excess waste generated, some of which threatens the planetary climate. Canadians live in the midst of abundance, in one of the wealthiest countries in the world, during the most productive era in the history of human endeavour. Yet the use of food banks continues to rise, along with child poverty. People are encouraged to feel insecure. No job, employers tell us, is secure anymore.

This sense of insecurity is magnified in the poorer countries around the world. When CEP was founded, fourteen million children were dying every year before

only twenty workers on the night shift.

Still, Richard and the rest of the executive were not prepared to let the changing technology push people they had worked with for so many years out the door. "We had a moral and social imperative to do something to try and keep as many workers as possible in the factory."

What Local 11 did was negotiate a deal with management to save ten jobs. Some three-quarters of the members of the local voted for the reduction in work time. Although the shorter hours resulted in a small net loss in pay for the workers, Richard decided it was worth it. The local succeeded in getting the employer to pick up the benefit costs. The benefits to the community were also well worth it. Ten jobs at roughly $50,000 each meant an extra half a million dollars remained in the community.

Ten jobs at roughly $50,000 each meant an extra half a million dollars remained in the community.

"It's helping a lot of people," Richard said. "Not just the workers, but everybody around here. We feel good about that."

CEP is a union that takes its community responsibility seriously. It defines that responsibility as everything from sponsoring amateur hockey teams to promoting a social vision of sharing the work and the wealth. Shorter hours are an integral part of a community vision that has spanned generations of workers.

"Older employees managed to save my job," Paul Raby said. "If I have the opportunity to do the same, I would not hesitate in voting for a decrease in the number of work hours to save a younger person's job." △

The members of ► Local 855 in Hinton, Alta., don't want to miss seeing their children grow up. Sean McDonald was the 2001 winner of the local's annual family fishing derby.

the age of five. That year the United Nation's *Human Development Report* showed that the richest 20 per cent of the world's people had incomes sixty times greater than the poorest 20 per cent. The disparity had doubled in thirty years.

It is a tragic paradox, more dramatic to be sure than forcing people to work fourteen months a year while so many others have no work at all. But both paradoxes remind us of the famous observation that Mahatma Gandhi once made. Gandhi's point is pertinent to any discussion of globalization: the world has enough for everyone's need, but not for everyone's greed.

In the end, the CEP workers at Lafarge ended their strike after six months, having secured an agreement from the employer to increase the workforce by 17 per cent. They also got an 11 per cent pay increase over 3.5 years, the first retirement bonus plan ever negotiated at Lafarge, and job security guarantees throughout the life of the agreement. As for the cement company's demand that they would always be on call, carrying pagers seven days a week, sixteen hours a day, the local succeeded in getting that reduced to weekends. For local president Doug Chisolm, this was a "bit of a compromise," but it was more than offset by the job creation gained in the new collective agreement – plus the boost that the whole struggle gave to Local 2190. "Senior people with twenty-five years told me during the strike that they had never seen the local so strong. And that's the way we went back."

Assuming a leadership role

IF SARNIA IS THE CITY where CEP's pioneering efforts on the shorter hours front had the greatest effect, the union in Saskatchewan has been in the shorter hours vanguard on the provincial level.

Saskatchewan telephone workers have been organized since 1945, when they were quick to take advantage of the labour-friendly organizing laws passed after Tommy Douglas's CCF government came to office the year before. Theirs was the very first certification of public employees under the new government's new labour laws. A generation later, with Allan Blakeney's NDP government in power, clerical and administrative workers at SaskTel moved to a 35-hour workweek and technicians lowered their weekly hours to 37.3. By the turn of the century, the reduced workweek had become a way of life, second nature to the Western phone workers.

Philip Bray, who does plant maintenance at SaskTel, enjoys having a long weekend every second weekend. "It's an extra day to get things done and spend time with each other," he said. His partner is one of the federal government workers who have taken advantage of the shorter hours trend. "I look forward to it," Philip said. "We do more things together on that day than on the weekend."

Philip acknowledged that not everyone in Local 2S wants a shorter workweek. Some of the membership would rather have more money than more time. Today many people in general remain caught up in the hurry-up ethic of turbo capitalism. SaskTel claims that the shorter workweek gives the company staffing headaches, while CEP suggests that the company can always hire more people. But a clear consensus does exist on the issue. "A majority of people have told us they would walk the picket line before going back to longer hours," Philip said.

CEP has assumed a leadership role in promoting shorter hours within the broader labour movement, and Saskatchewan is no exception. When the Saskatchewan Federation of Labour organized its "Get a Life" conference to develop strategies for reduced work time and family-friendly workplaces, two of the five speakers (Mike Verdiel of Powell River and Julie White of the national office) came from CEP.

Along with reprinting CEP's Resolution G-12 on shorter hours, the conference report explained the nuts and bolts of everything from payroll structure to job-creation strategies. It emphasized where unions are doing well on the work time issue and where they are falling short, and it situated the struggle for shorter hours in the international context. The writers used CEP's B.C. research findings to show how it would cost employers less to hire more workers than to make their existing employees work more overtime. In the end the landmark SFL report turned out to be an invaluable resource for trade unionists who want to learn more about the issue. △

> "A majority of people have told us they would walk the picket line before going back to longer hours."
> • PHILIP BRAY

"It's time to look out for the other guy"

THE MILL AT POWELL RIVER, the oldest newsprint mill west of Ontario, has been decimated by layoffs. In the mid-1960s the huge mill had ten newsprint machines. As late as 1989, when Mike Verdiel became president of Local 76, some fifteen hundred people worked at the mill. By 2002 the number had shrunk to about a third of that. CEP continued to struggle to keep members working and the community vibrant. One of its tools has been cutting both overtime and the length of the workweek.

"Unions are always accused of looking out for ourselves," said Mike, at forty-seven one of the youngest pipefitters at the mill. "Here we're trying to reduce the workweek to keep people employed, and not just our own members."

"The extra time off is good if you want to be an active father," Willy Roberts explains. "You get to play a lot of roles that were traditionally held only by the mother."

In a union town like Powell River, a job loss at the main employer has big ripple effects. Several schools have shut, forcing teachers to leave. When union jobs go, so too do jobs with good benefit packages. This means less business for dentists and chiropractors and the people who work for them.

"It's time to look out for the other guy," said millwright Larry Cole, who supported a 2002 reduction in working hours. The introduction of a new schedule of thirty-seven and a third hours saved eighteen jobs. "There are just not enough hours in the day trying to get the shorter workweek," Mike said, without apparent irony.

The commitment to cutting hours at Local 76 goes back to CEP's first days. When the local changed its bylaws as part of the switch to the new CEP, it decided to charge dues on all hours worked — including overtime. The membership voted unanimously for the idea. In 1998 the local went to forty hours from forty-two, creating twenty-two full-time jobs. When the time came for the workers on the West Coast to go to a schedule of thirty-seven and a third hours, CEP

K. NEWMAN

◀ *Log loader and boom boat, Powell River, B.C. The mill at Powell River has been decimated by layoffs.*

"We're trying to reduce the workweek to keep people employed."
• MIKE VERDIEL, PRESIDENT, LOCAL 76

already had a template ready on the East Coast. Mike made a trip to Dalhousie, N.B., to learn how they did it there.

As a result, Local 76 has used the new shorter hours schedule to address another problem festering at Canadian mills. A dozen new apprenticeships have opened up in Powell River. CEP has been criticizing employers for their neglect in training skilled trades. Local 76 has found an innovative way to promote shorter hours while simultaneously boosting apprenticeships.

"I was successful in applying for an apprenticeship due to the fact that our union has taken steps towards saving jobs," said Willy Roberts, who had long wanted to become a skilled trades worker. Willy was already enjoying the benefits of shorter hours.

Both his girls play soccer and softball and do highland dancing, and now he has more time to help them out, more time with the family generally.

"The extra time off is good if you want to be an active father," he explains. "You get to play a lot of roles that were traditionally held only by the mother."

For Mike Verdiel, if he didn't spend all that time agitating for shorter hours, he would be volunteering somewhere else. He does it because he believes in what he's doing and in what his union is doing.

"It's something we have to do as a society, and it's something the union has to push," he said. "The CEP is stepping out in front and identifying ourselves as a union working towards full employment for Canadians. The same with medicare. It's important that we stay in the forefront on issues where everyone can benefit." ◬

▼ *A dozen new apprenticeships have opened up in Powell River. Local 76 has found an innovative way to promote shorter hours while simultaneously boosting apprenticeships.*

NEWMAN

CHAPTER TEN

Appliances, drywall, and insulation:
THREE WORKPLACES IN QUEBEC

TELEVISION STUDIOS in Toronto and telephone trucks in Sherbrooke. Oil refineries in Edmonton and Saint John. Pulp and paper towns in Northern Ontario and Quebec's Mauricie. These are the workplaces that come to mind at the mention of a union called the Communications, Energy and Paperworkers. These are the people who bring you the news, from the newsprint to the daily paper and the nightly newscast. They'll install your phone line and refine the gas for your car.

But if you're renovating your kitchen, you might also look to CEP members and the products they produce. And you would not have to look further than Montreal and three riverside factories where they make the insulation to keep your kitchen warm, the drywall to cover the insulation, and the appliances you might want for the renovation. Each of these plants was the site of an important challenge confronted – successfully – by CEP locals.

▲ Camco, Westroc, and Owens Corning. Each of these plants was the site of an important challenge confronted – successfully – by CEP locals. Brian Payne addresses a rally of Westroc strike supporters.

127

The Camco strike

BACK IN 1940 the corner of Dickson and Notre Dame in east-end Montreal was the perfect place for a wartime factory. It was so close to the riverside docks that the heavy tanks could be loaded directly onto freighters for the journey to England and, eventually, the battlefields of France, Holland, and Germany.

Some sixty years later the plant's output of dishwashers and clothes dryers is shipped out by truck, but the gritty industrial area is still heavy with traffic going to and from the nearby port. As trucks loaded with containers – Maersk Sealand, P&O Nedlloyd, Hanjin, CN – make the tight turn off Notre Dame and north on Dickson, they grind their way through at least four gears. It isn't Montreal's quietest neighbourhood.

It got even noisier for ten weeks in 2001. Each time a truck turned the corner and the driver noticed the CEP picket signs, he gave a long, enthusiastic blast of solidarity on his air horn. The pickets from Local 501 at Camco – a nominally independent company controlled by General Electric – responded with raised fists and smiles. They were used to working in the din of metal-on-metal and air tools, and they figured it was only fair for the plant managers in the upstairs offices to get their share. Call it the Democratization of Noise.

Most of the workers at the Camco plant have over twenty years of service, so when they voted to strike they remembered the three-week walkout in 1980, when the local suffered a defeat. "There was a psychological barrier there," said local president Alain Leduc. "The members still had some sad memories of 1980."

The Camco strike. ▶
Each time a truck turned the corner and the driver noticed the CEP picket signs, he gave a long, enthusiastic blast of solidarity on his air horn.

Alain recalled the late 1980s and early 1990s as a period when the local lived through a series of management-inspired plans that he described with the English word "partnership": joint committees; work teams; work reorganization. The employer always seemed to frame these efforts with a sense of urgency and a discussion of the need to keep the plant in Montreal. Jobs were at stake. These were, after all, the years of free trade, NAFTA, and early mentions of something called "globalization." What's more, the depression of the early 1990s hit the working class in east-end Montreal particularly hard.

By the time that bargaining reached an impasse in 2001, management was muttering darkly about the plant being relocated to Mexico. Alain knew that they didn't make dishwashers and dryers down there because he'd toured the *maquiladoras* and attended international meetings with workers from other parts of General Electric's global production line. But he also knew that it didn't mean that the giant conglomerate was not capable of making these appliances down south.

All of which put the employer's fashionable partnership plans in a new light. Alain called the whole recipe "the myth of collaboration." Although it is possible to work with the employer on issues of common interest, he said, there can never be any sort of joint management for a simple reason. "We are not the owners of this factory. And when they talk about the survival of the factory on the backs of the workers, we aren't going anywhere near that. There's no possible partnership."

A case of spontaneous combustion

BY SPRING 2001 the CEP members at Camco had obviously put the defeat of 1980 behind them. A two-day lockout and an employer demand for wall-to-wall concessions on pensions and the drug benefit plan spurred them on. The workers believed they had no choice but to meet the challenge. They gave their negotiating committee an 85.6 per cent strike mandate on April 1. As it turned out, the joke on management went well beyond the noise of the air horns blasting away down on the street.

Three weeks into the strike the employer withdrew its demands for concessions and asked CEP to hold another vote. But by this time the membership was in no mood to accept the status quo. "We didn't go out on strike after twenty years just to keep what we already had," Alain said. "The members wanted to make some gains."

The conflict continued as the weather warmed up. The local leadership's normal efforts to maintain unity were challenged by a nasty company

The pickets from Local 501 at Camco … responded with raised fists and smiles. They were used to working in the din of metal-on-metal and air tools, and they figured it was only fair for the plant managers in the upstairs offices to get their share. Call it the Democratization of Noise.

letter-writing campaign. On a half-dozen occasions over the course of the strike the appliance workers received courier packages at home. The letters – which local activists dubbed PEUR-O-LETTRES (*peur* being French for "fear") – were designed to spook the members and their families. The messages claimed that Local 501 was keeping information from the employees, that Camco had demanded no concessions, and that the local leadership was afraid of a vote.

This prompted CEP to come up with an innovative way of turning back the employer's offensive. The Camco activists put out the usual leaflets and talked things up on the picket line, but Pierre Auger, a former local president, also created a Local 501 website that he constantly updated, posting the latest news and countering the company propaganda. This new strategy also allowed the members to e-mail their comments and ideas back to the leadership, which helped keep everyone in closer touch. A few weeks after the CEP site went up, the company, desperately struggling to catch up, established a site of its own.

"We had a little war there," Alain said. "It was one of our first Internet strikes. We had just entered a new century and along with it a new level of struggle using new technology."

The strike ended in June with improvements in the pension plan and wage increases. The first day back at work everyone wore the CEP T-shirts and baseball caps that had become their trademark symbols over the course of the walkout. Having faced down one of the world's biggest transnational corporations, the workers entered the old plant singing a victory song.

Having faced down one of the world's biggest transnational corporations, the Camco workers entered the old plant singing a victory song. ▼

◀ *Westroc employees were sick of making changes to schedules, and were angry about an inferior pension plan. Management was confident that CEP would never take them on in a strike. They were wrong.*

The old fears left over from the previous strike had evaporated, giving way to a new sense of unity and strength. During a searing heat wave a few weeks after the return to work, the temperature in the plant climbed to record levels. When air-conditioned managers refused to agree to requests from the shop floor for extra breaks, the assembly line came to an immediate halt. It was a spontaneous job action on the part of the workers, not something that the local planned. By the end of the workday the employer had capitulated, agreeing to the additional time off.

Rocking the boat at Westroc

SAINTE-CATHERINE IS LOCATED in a good place to manufacture a heavy product like drywall. The St. Lawrence widens just downriver from the Mercier bridge, and ships can dock right beside the Westroc plant, unloading their bulk cargoes of Nova Scotia gypsum. From there it's like making a huge biscuit. The gypsum is mixed into a greyish pudding-like filling and spread on a sheet of paper moving at 210 feet per minute. Another sheet of paper gets rolled onto the filling and within an hour the finished product – four by eight pieces of drywall – has been dried and is being stacked ten pallets high.

A labourer at Westroc starts at $18 an hour. It's a union shop. It is also a workplace where the local union made a remarkable comeback after getting beaten up by management in 1991, just before the formation of CEP. Back then, as soon as the workers decided to hold a one-day study session, the hard-nosed plant management decided to lock them out. The lockout lasted four months, during which time the workers even wondered whether the company would close the factory for good. Claude Roy, who would later become president of the local at Westroc, described the experience as "very unsettling."

Quebec Federation of ► *Labour construction workers agreed to place an embargo on all Westroc products, refusing to use them.*

COPYRIGHT: SERGE JONGUÉ • PHOTO: IMRE MURA

"We have a union when people stand up for their principles. I believe that being a union member means standing up for yourself."
• LOUIS TREMBLAY

"Employees said, 'We will return. Under the employer's rules, but we will return.'"

Eight years later the employer was still confident that the workers, now members of CEP Local 134Q, would never take them on in a strike. They wouldn't even stage a study session. It was perhaps for this reason that Westroc management decided to bring in unilateral scheduling changes. The employer also refused to make any changes to a pension plan that the eighty workers knew lagged far behind the plans that the company had in place at its operations in Toronto and Calgary. All this in addition to maintaining a hard line on the shop floor in day-to-day dealings with the workers. Westroc believed that it still had the upper hand, that the events of 1991 were still fresh in the minds of the members of the new union.

They were wrong. Things had changed. According to Claude, "Employees were sick of making changes to schedules." They were also angry about having a pension plan that was inferior to the one that the same company maintained for workers making the same product for the same market. With the $200 a week that the CEP Defense Fund would pay to each striker, things would be better on the picket line. Local 134Q voted to strike.

As electrician Louis Tremblay put it, "We have a union when people stand up for their principles. I believe that being a union member means standing up for yourself."

The workers stood up for nine months after the walkout started in April 2000. CEP members from Quebec established contact with the unions at Westroc plants in Ontario and Alberta, receiving considerable financial support. (All in all 134Q got $30,000 over the course of the strike.) At the beginning of June a group of strikers travelled to Toronto, where they set up pickets in front of the Westroc plant and forced the company to stop production for twenty-four hours.

This prompted the company to change its bargaining position slightly. The local held a membership meeting to discuss an offer that was in effect not much of an offer at all.

"The employees answered 'no' after a period of four months," Claude Roy said.

The strike continued into the fall, at which point CEP made an appeal to the construction unions in the Quebec Federation of Labour. The drywall workers figured that construction sites would be a good pressure point on their employer. The construction workers agreed to place an embargo on all Westroc products, refusing to use them. Which caused the company to pay attention.

"The company said 'We're going to lose our clients and our market share,'" Claude recalled. "From that point on they truly committed themselves to serious negotiations."

In December Local 134Q ratified a deal that contained none of the concessions originally tabled by the employer. Instead, it gave them 1.75 per cent wage increases and a 20 per cent increase in the pension plan. It also gave them something intangible.

Looking back on the strike a year later, Louis Tremblay said that the atmosphere in the plant had changed. "Current management is much more respectful of blue-collar employees than they have been in the past."

◀ *The Westroc workers stood up for their principles for nine months after the walkout started in April 2000.*

Owens Corning: "This is one of our shining moments"

THEY MAKE HOME INSULATION at a CEP-organized factory at Candiac, just a few kilometres downriver from the Westroc plant at Sainte-Catherine. The workers at Owens Corning were off work for a long spell just before the Westroc workers went on strike. But Local 821 had no choice in the matter.

In some ways, Local 821 is typical of many other locals in CEP. It consists of a group of middle-aged workers, the average age being forty-eight. The lowest seniority is twenty years. Most of the membership is male. They are all aware of employer talk of the need to be competitive. They are even more aware than most that the plant could shut down. That's because it did. The plant only reopened after CEP and the Quebec Solidarity Fund stepped in with some money and advice, saving eighty-four jobs in Candiac.

"Experts from the fund and the CEP gave us a great deal of help in this regard," said Yves Dumont, president of local 821.

Things have changed since the reopening in 1999. The plant now only makes home insulation, having shed the money-losing industrial insulation production that was dragging it down. The company has trimmed the management staff along with the union workforce, which stood at 211 when the plant closed the year before. Yves talked approvingly of the new attitudes on the job. In the wake of the union-driven reopening the company had opted for a new, team-style approach that placed its remaining local managers in glass-walled offices next to the production floor. The offices upstairs sit empty, including the "Salle Clouseau." As a way of promoting its trademark pink insulation, Owens Corning purchased the rights to use that name from the people who made the movie *The Pink Panther*.

"I believe that people on both sides learned from that plant closing," explained Yves, who wore one of the black shirts with a pink-panther logo that the company had distributed when it proclaimed the Candiac plant Factory of the Year in 2000. "The employees mellowed a great deal."

The members of Local 821 went through a lot to get to the point where they were back on the job. In the years before the closure there had been rumours that the plant was on the chopping block. Relations with management were not good, nor was the plant's health and safety record. They had a high accident rate, perhaps the highest of all the plants operated by Owens Corning. According to Yves, "It had almost become a first aid unit, which created a great deal of tension on the factory floor."

The dismal health and safety record, aging equipment, poor management decisions, bad union-employer relations, and problematic product lines all

In the years before the closure there had been rumours that the plant was on the chopping block. Relations with management were not good, nor was the plant's health and safety record.

added up to low productivity. In late 1997 Owens Corning announced that it would be closing the plant in April 1998.

The reaction was muted. Expecting trouble of some sort, the company had taken all manner of precautionary measures to prevent disgruntled workers from retaliating. As it turned out, there was no worker revolt, no vandalism. The two hundred-plus workers were just too stunned about losing their jobs to do much of anything.

For Yves, this revealed that the workers were not, in fact, troublemakers, that they had their heads well affixed to their shoulders. And it also stood them in good stead when it came to the decision to reopen the plant. "We are very proud of that. This is one of our shining moments, in my opinion."

Once the plant was closed, CEP and the Solidarity Fund swung into action with a research team that investigated the Candiac situation closely, assessing the facility's strengths and weaknesses. They discovered that things were not all that bad. The plant needed an injection of capital and a change of product line, but it was certainly not a hopeless situation. Their profitability studies must have been right on, or otherwise Owens Corning would not have agreed to negotiate a deal, which was backed up by an investment of $7.5 million from the fund. The Candiac plant was reopened fourteen months after the company had decided it had produced its last batt of fibreglass insulation there. CEP and the Solidarity Fund had saved the day.

"I think that the Solidarity Fund and the union make a really strong team," said Yves. "Both of them work hand in hand. If the union needs financial support, the fund proves to be an extremely worthy ally."

"I think that the Solidarity Fund and the union make a really strong team," said Yves Dumont. "Both of them work hand in hand. If the union needs financial support, the fund proves to be an extremely worthy ally."

◀ *The Candiac plant was reopened fourteen months after the company had decided it had produced its last batt of fiberglass insulation there. CEP and the Solidarity Fund had saved the day.*

Local 821 still faces challenges, even though it managed to preserve 40 per cent of the $18 an hour production jobs and the Candiac plant won the Owens Corning Factory of the Year award again in 2000. Like many other CEP workplaces where the people are pushing fifty, keeping up with the physical pace of fast production during twelve-hour shifts is getting more and more difficult for the workers. The local would also like to add some new jobs, providing work for younger people and more security for the workers who managed to keep their jobs.

As he walked past the mission statement with the pink-panther logo, Yves also said that on a clear day you can still see the tiny dust particles when the sunbeams stream through the windows. Asked if he had any words of wisdom about the Solidarity Fund for other CEP members, he replied that lots of people in Quebec who have the money to invest in an RRSP put it into the fund.

"That money actually serves to promote and protect Quebec-based jobs, which is a huge asset and very important as well. I think that if the fund had not been there, we would not be here today."

CHAPTER ELEVEN

Canadian Broadcasting Corporation · Société Radio-(

W. SAUNDERS

How CEP became the "media union"

OUTSIDE TORONTO, IT WAS A JOKE: "Remember the time Mel Lastman called in the army when it snowed in January."

Toronto reporter Ka Hung Wong may recall it as one of the Toronto mayor's gaffes, but chances are he will also remember it as the excuse they used when they tried to fire him for literally going the extra mile to make sure his paper provided meaningful coverage of the storm.

He could have stayed in the office. The *Sing Tao Daily*'s new owner, Torstar Corp., through its daily *The Toronto Star*, had lots of photos of the snowstorm that was buffeting the city. But K.H. wanted something relevant to his own paper's readers. Even though the storm was so bad that one of the other reporters hadn't been able to get out of his driveway, K.H. drove across the snow-clogged downtown to take photographs of the scene at Spadina and Dundas, the heart of Toronto's main Chinatown. He was just doing his job, and he didn't think about it again until the employer alleged that he had not covered the storm adequately and that was why they had fired him.

The day K.H. was fired he had three stories in the paper (including two on its first news page). *Sing Tao* claimed he was "disruptive" and "not a team player."

▲ *The Vancouver Raging Grannies support CBC regional programming. So does CEP, Canada's media union.*

Ka Hung Wong, Ray ▲
Chan, and Rose Cho
worked hard on the
campaign to organize
the Sing Tao *newspaper.*
The Local 87M members
at the Chinese-language
daily spent seven weeks
on the picket line
in 2000.

As it happened, K.H. had been organizing the *Sing Tao* staff, signing the nervous sales reps and editors up as members of Local 87M. When the union took the case to the Ontario Labour Relations Board (OLRB), the employer's argument was so pitiful that all it could muster was puzzling excuses like the snowstorm incident.

The OLRB members, flabbergasted, pointed out that the company's "patently false and after-the-fact excuses" showed that it wanted to "hide the real reason" for firing such a conscientious reporter. That reason, of course, was that he was organizing a union.

Dog bites man. Boss fires worker for unionizing. It's a story as old as the hills. What made it exceptional was who was signing the cards. "*Sing Tao* is the first ever Chinese media outlet in Canada to form a union," said K.H. "It's an extremely important milestone for the history of Canadian Chinese union organizing and for labour history in general."

Like most such firsts in labour history, it did not come easily. Secretive meetings in donut shops. Intimidation and firing. A long first-contract strike.

The organizing started when reporter Ray Chan was covering the Ontario legislature for *Sing Tao*. In 1998 Ray got to talking with Martin Mittelstaedt, a *Globe and Mail* reporter and long-time activist in the Southern Ontario Newspaper Guild (SONG), by this time CEP Local 87M. This was just after Torstar Corp. had bought *Sing Tao*, Toronto's biggest Chinese daily, from a Hong Kong company. Discontent over the allocation of bonus pay was simmering at the paper.

At first Ray and K.H. concentrated their efforts on the editorial staff, but they soon started to sign up people in sales, clerical, and production. The local also hired a Chinese-speaking organizer to help out, and it all paid off. By May 2000 the forty editorial staff had voted by over 90 per cent to join CEP. They were soon followed by seventy other workers. But *Sing Tao* and Torstar had no desire to see CEP gain a foothold in the sector. They fired K.H. even before the bargaining unit was certified and forced the new members, none of whom had any union experience, into a strike situation. The *Sing Tao* workers responded by walking out and spending seven weeks on the picket line, eventually winning a solid, three-year collective agreement.

By the time the strike got underway, K.H. was back on the job. He had also had a friendly argument with 87M executive officer Howard Law. K.H. adamantly refused to take the money that the OLRB had ordered the employer to pay him as compensation for unjust dismissal. Howard insisted that he had earned it, that the company had put him through the wringer.

"K.H. , you lost money," Howard said.

"I didn't go into this to get money," K.H. told him. K.H. wanted to give the money to the union.

"The CEP was extremely helpful," K.H. explained. "They spent a lot of money even before the local was set up. I was too ashamed to take any compensation. The union made a lot of effort and it paid off."

K.H. cashed the cheque and gave the money to the local, which put it into an educational trust fund. "That's the kind of guy he is," said Howard.

Organizing broadcasters: a campaign "with reach"

WHEN 88 PER CENT of his members voted to join CEP in 1994, Gord Hunter of NABET was a bit surprised. He had expected a Yes vote, but the margin was a bit overwhelming. "I must have gone through thirty ballots before I got a No," he said.

The members of NABET – the National Association of Broadcast Employees and Technicians – knew they were headed for tough times. "Our strike fund was pretty small," said Marc-Philippe Laurin of the CBC in Ottawa. "We were starting to think that maybe we would not be able to survive as NABET."

"Sing Tao is the first ever Chinese media outlet in Canada to form a union," said Ka Hung Wong. *"It's an extremely important milestone for the history of Canadian Chinese union organizing and for labour history in general."*

◄ *Founding president Don Holder supports striking newspaper workers with CEP national rep Joy Langan (former compositor and former NDP Member of Parliament).*

The camera people, studio technicians, set designers, and carpenters wanted a bigger union with more resources. They chose CEP because it was a new Canadian union with fresh energy, one that they hoped they could help shape.

After promising stable funding for the CBC in the 1993 election, the Chrétien Liberals were beginning a series of cuts that would remove $400 million, or 27 per cent of the public broadcaster's budget. The camera people, studio technicians, set designers, and carpenters wanted a bigger union with more resources. They chose CEP because it was a new Canadian union with fresh energy, one that they hoped they could help shape.

NABET was soon joined in CEP by newspaper and magazine people who were also looking for organizational strength. The companies that dominated their industries had lots of changes in mind, but behind all the hype about the information superhighway and convergence, some old realities and the same old social relations remained: speed-up; more with less; bigger employers, fewer employees. The agenda was full when CEP activists representing seventeen thousand members convened for the first meeting of the union's Media Council in 1995.

Between 1991 and 1996 Southam cut its workforce in half, eliminating six thousand positions; and by spring 1996 Southam newspapers had been taken over by Conrad Black, a rich fellow who liked to use big words almost as much as he disliked unions. CEP teamed up with the Council of Canadians to challenge Black's takeover of Southam in the courts, arguing that allowing too many media outlets to fall into too few hands was bad for democracy. It was an argument that had been heard before two royal commissions on media concentration in the past twenty-five years. Both commissions found that press freedom was only meaningful if press ownership was widely dispersed. Both were ignored by Ottawa.

CEP lost its court case challenging corporate concentration in the media, but its point was well taken. A study of bias in the newspapers revealed that coverage of labour issues in *The Vancouver Sun*'s editorial pages fell from 11.4 per cent in 1991 to 0 per cent in 1996. Similarly, the *Ottawa Citizen* had no labour coverage in 1996. In the union city of Windsor, Ont., in 1991 about 21 per cent of all front-page items in the Southam-owned *Windsor Star* had dealt with labour issues. Some five years later the front-page coverage of labour issues was down to 1.8 per cent. By 1996 the *Windsor Star*'s editorial page devoted more space to sports than to labour, women's, and Aboriginal issues combined.

The diversity of media ownership in Ontario was further threatened in 1995 when Mike Harris's Conservatives took over. Immediately after becoming premier, Harris declared that he was prepared to privatize TVO and TFO, the publicly owned English- and French-language educational broadcasters. He stacked the board with cronies who favoured selling the place. It looked like

P. KEIGHLEY

◄ The campaign tapped into the wide public support enjoyed by TVO/TFO, mobilizing people who did not want their children numbed by programming whose purpose was to sell action figures and Nintendo games.

Ontario's public broadcaster would suffer the fate of Alberta's Access, sold to the private sector for a dollar. But it didn't happen.

"Our little local could not have done it alone – no way," said Marj Cromb, who worked on the CEP's TVO Matters! campaign and later became president of Local 72M. "We didn't have the contacts or the money. We couldn't have done it without the support of the larger union."

TVO and TFO produce educational programming that is available without cable to most every citizen of Ontario. They remained in public hands because of some deft politicking by a union committed to public broadcasting and a management that shared that commitment. The union campaign tapped into the wide public support enjoyed by TVO/TFO, mobilizing people who did not want their children to be numbed by programming whose purpose was to sell action figures and Nintendo games. They preferred commercial-free television designed to teach and entertain children. TVO's weekday children's shows account for a quarter of its total viewing hours, and Marj Cromb recalled learning how to calculate area while watching a TVO children's show.

Local 72M vice-president Larry Currie and national representative Dave Lewington brought Marj into the campaign and together they employed CEP's provincewide network of members to get their message out. They had a video, buttons, pamphlets, news releases, speakers, and advertisements. People who had donated money to TVO/TFO (and had voted Conservative) were an important constituency, and soon politicians were being yelled at about the proposed privatization. Parent councils at schools got copies of the video, which contained clips from TVO/TFO shows. So too did community groups and

DAVID CLIMENHAGA

Canadian writer ▲
Margaret Atwood walks
the union walk with
strikers on the Calgary
Herald *picket line.*

riding associations. It was, as the advertisers say, a campaign with tremendous "reach."

The organizers were ready by the time the government staged its public consultations on privatization. Even though participants could react only to six predetermined questions, the Tory consultants came back with a report of "clear public opposition" to the proposed sale of TVO/TFO. During the CEP campaign, polling showed that the number of people opposed to the sell-off rose from 48 per cent of those polled to 60 per cent in just three months. In 1998 the Harris government, anticipating an election within the year, announced that TVO/TFO would remain a public agency.

It was a "strategic coup," according to a study in the *Canadian Journal of Communication.* Carleton University journalism professor Kirsten Kozolanka described Local 72M's campaign as a "remarkable effort from a union local in an organization that had been downsized from 565 employees in 1993 to 417 in 1997."

"Journalism under attack"

THE *CALGARY HERALD* had never been known as a bastion of left-wing thinking. It was a traditional Southam paper with a conservative newsroom, but things changed after Conrad Black bought Southam. New managers arrived, and reporters were told that it was a very good idea to contact Reform Party members of parliament on just about any issue vaguely related to politics. They began to notice that quotes from the Reformers had a way of getting placed high up in their stories. Civic boosterism was turned up a notch. One reporter was even called on the carpet for writing a critical story about the Calgary Flames.

Although the paper had no union, it did have a salary grid. Suddenly people recently hired were getting paid less than the grid stipulated. One senior manager began walking around the newsroom telling senior staff people, "You know, we could hire two young crackerjacks for what we're paying you."

In 1998 the staff at the *Herald* were taking union talk seriously. The CEP's Gail Lem and Dave Coles, however, took things slowly, waiting patiently until the previously unthinkable – a union at the most conservative paper in Canada's most conservative province – looked possible. By autumn twenty-five people had signed cards, and on the Friday of Thanksgiving weekend the union set up at a hotel near the *Herald*'s remote location in northeast Calgary. The phones got busy. By Saturday night enough of the "yes" and "yes-maybe" people had signed cards that Local 115A was set to go. A majority of reporters, editors, photographers, and librarians were on side. By the time the "noes" were called and management learned what was happening, it was too late. The *Herald* was caught flatfooted. The certification vote was 75 per cent in favour. Just as the organizing drive was taking place, Conrad Black's Hollinger company was launching his financially disastrous *National Post*, the greatest money pit in the history of Canadian journalism.

The subsequent strike did not go as smoothly. The union was defeated, but in the process CEP showed its members that it would back them all the way. The fight became not only a first-contract dispute but also a symbolic battle against monolithic corporate control of the media.

The strike happened because Southam was simply unwilling to bargain in good faith. The two sides would spend hours haggling over a word or phrase. The employer would not agree to a basic seniority clause. After ten months of fruitless talks, Local 115A got a strike mandate from the members, but on November 8, before they could walk out, the company locked them out, deploying an intimidating squad of rent-a-cops. The law protected the employer with severe picketing restrictions.

"Just about no one in the newsroom had ever participated in this sort of thing," recalled Andy Marshall, a reporter with thirteen years at the *Herald*. "We received staggering support from other locals, especially 87M in Ontario and 2000 in B.C. That, plus the level of support from unions in Calgary and across the country, just amazed us."

The fight became not only a first-contract dispute but also a symbolic battle against monolithic corporate control of the media.

◀ *"The level of support from unions in Calgary and across the country just amazed us."*

• ANDY MARSHALL, *CALGARY HERALD* REPORTER

Andy had helped with the organizing and found himself in the position of being a leader of a local strike that attracted national attention. He was the one who approached Black when the magnate was attending a meeting in Calgary, urging him to negotiate an end to the dispute. Black responded with a tirade, telling Andy that the union had better return to work or he would wait them out for two years. "That was when he referred to us as gangrenous limbs that needed to be amputated."

Being insulted by Black wasn't what upset Andy. The man was, after all, a caricature of a business bullhorn whom someone would have had to invent had he not sprung unbidden from Upper Canada College. What really irked Andy was that someone in Black's position could openly flout the law by saying he had no intention of bargaining at the same time as the CEP members were being forced to kowtow to every legal technicality on the picket line. A top Alberta civil servant acknowledged to Andy that Black and Hollinger were breaking the law, but said there was no political will to do anything about it. "I'm still shocked by that," Andy said. "The government would do nothing about people breaking the law."

As the months dragged on, support for the strike withered away, with a few people returning to work over the winter. Alberta's boss-friendly labour laws allowed the paper to keep publishing a diminished version throughout. By July, ninety-three strikers voted to take a company offer of a severance package rather than return to work at the *Herald*. On one level it was a defeat, and a bitter one at that. But it was also another sign that in the first few years of its existence CEP would not back down in the face of intransigence or intimidation by employers, no matter how big or powerful: Abitibi, Petro-Canada, Bell Canada, the CBC, Irving Oil, Fletcher Challenge, Conrad Black.

"There is no question in the minds of our membership," Brian Payne said, "that we have an obligation to stand together and take on those corporations and make sure our members are backed up in those struggles. We tend to represent people at the big players in the economy. And those employers know full well where we stand if they try to take advantage of us."

CEP's organizing efforts in Alberta continued apace during the *Calgary Herald* strike. At IPEX, an Edmonton plastic pipe manufacturer, 150 new members joined the union. A few months after the strike ended, CEP organizer Bill Kolba signed up fourteen hundred workers at the Calgary Catholic School Board. The nasty confrontation at the *Herald* had reminded potential members in Alberta and everywhere else in the country that if they were looking for a union that would only choose its fights according to those it might win and would run away from the ones it might lose, they should not

> Adversity is a great unifier, strengthening the social glue that binds people together. These are critical ingredients for any culture – family, workplace, union, nation.

sign a CEP card. But if they wanted an organization that backed its members right to the end, they would find a home there.

Making a racket at the CBC

BY 1999 THE CEP members at the CBC had become fed up with the years of systematic staff reductions brought on by Ottawa's attacks on public broadcasting. They had joined CEP five years earlier to obtain the tools to take on the employer.

In 1999 they were ready to do so, and the result was a 10 per cent pay increase over three years. Some two hundred people who had been on a forty-hour week had their work time reduced to 38.75 hours with no loss of pay. New contract language resulted in forty-six new jobs. There were better severance and recall provisions. The ratification vote was over 90 per cent in favour of the deal, ending a seven-week walkout.

Strikes are never easy, and the CBC dispute was no exception. "It's not a good feeling, being on strike," said Marc-Philippe Laurin, an Ottawa radio technician who helped to organize the action. "But at the same time it did wonders for the solidarity of our membership. They were tighter than I have ever seen them."

In 1999 members at the CBC were ready to take on the employers, and the result was a 10 per cent pay increase over three years. Some two hundred people who had been on a forty-hour week had their work time reduced to 38.75 hours with no loss of pay.

R. HATFIELD

◀ *CEP vice-president, media, Peter Murdoch walks the union walk with Marc-Philippe Laurin. "A lot of people were upset that management was mocking us. Son-of-a-gun! We just weren't going to put up with it."*

By 1999 the CEP ▶
members at the CBC
had become fed up
with the years of
systematic staff
reductions brought on
by Ottawa's attacks
on public broadcasting.

P. KEIGHLEY

Adversity is a great unifier, strengthening the social glue that binds people together. These are critical ingredients for any culture – family, workplace, union, nation. People look back and tell stories, and these stories have more staying power than the matter-of-fact accounts of the daily news that are so often described by journalists as "stories." The CEP members at CBC-Radio Canada in Ottawa tend to groan loudly when they hear that Marc-Philippe Laurin is about to tell his Noisy Thursday story. But he will tell it anyway, anytime, to anyone.

It started during Week Six of the strike, when someone suggested that the Ottawa strikers charter some buses and go to Toronto to shut down the big CBC Broadcast Centre there. "Why not just tell them we're going?" suggested someone else. So rumours of a mass picket on Front Street near the Sky Dome began circulating in both Ottawa and Toronto. Management somehow got wind of the plot and hired extra security guards. In Ottawa the managers could finally relax, and they even put up a mock picket line of their own. Then the strikers arrived.

"A lot of people were upset that management was mocking us," said Marc-Philippe. "Son-of-a-gun! We just weren't going to put up with it. So we got whistles, we got horns, we got metal garbage cans and hammers. And we just started making a racket you could hear at the CBC building in Toronto."

It turned into a bit of a picket line party. Management, their tempers frayed after six weeks of crossing a picket line and getting more stressed by doing the CEP members' work, was not amused. Several police cars pulled up at the line.

"The CBC has filed a complaint. The school across the street is very upset about the noise."

"Well, I'll go over and see what's going on."

Marc-Philippe trotted over to the school and, rather timidly, knocked on the main office door.

"I've heard that you complained to the CBC about the noise."

The woman sitting in the office looked perplexed. "What? We didn't complain to anyone," she said, peering out the window.

"Are you sure? We're making quite a racket out there and the police showed up."

"Sure I'm sure. The noise wouldn't bother us. We're a school for the deaf."

By 2002 another story had been circulating in the media union and beyond. It was about what CEP media vice-president Peter Murdoch called the "very empty balloon" that was "convergence" – the idea that the new technology of the Internet would somehow converge with older media such as newspapers and television to create a brave new world of communications. Rogers, Bell,

▲ *John Redekop, Local 82M, Winnipeg, and Augusta on the CBC picket line.*

and CanWest Global were all getting into the act. But, as it turned out, what the big media corporations managed to get into was debt. Nowhere was this more evident than in the Asper empire.

"The Asper regime is weighed down by a huge amount of debt," Peter said. "That creates absolutely no opportunity for enterprise. All we've seen have been drastic reductions in their newsrooms. And in television it's laughable. There has been an abandonment of any notion of local programming." It also means that media employers put pressure on CEP members and their collective agreements in their scramble for cash.

Against this background, the media union continued to press for the maintenance of journalistic standards (the issue at the heart of the *Calgary Herald* strike) by supporting public broadcasting and pressing for government action to curb the threat to democracy represented by corporate concentration in the private-sector media. There are clear parallels with the struggles of other unionized workers pushing back against the skewed logic of capital. "Journalists need to learn from nurses and teachers about the issue of maintaining standards in face of cuts," Peter said.

Peter Murdoch calls ▶
convergence a "very
empty balloon."
Peter Murdoch with
André Foucault at
a CBC rally on
Parliament Hill.

CHAPTER TWELVE

THE CASTLEGAR CITIZEN

David and Goliath revisited:
THE STORY OF THE *CASTLEGAR CITIZEN*

AT FIRST GLANCE the scene was no different from the everyday bustle in the office of any small newspaper. Deadline was fast approaching, and there was the usual undercurrent of controlled anxiety as pages took shape. The flats had to be shipped out earlier than usual because the printer was on the other side of the province.

The tense working silence was broken as the staff called out from behind the dun-coloured room dividers. "Who wants to proof page three?"

"I need to cut your story."

The stories deal with local happenings, from disputes over cat bylaws to the closure of the operating room because there is no surgeon in town. A twenty-three-year-old faller has been killed in a logging accident near Castlegar.

"Classifieds are clean!"

"I've got a hole on two. The sewer project story fits perfectly."

"How about this?" someone asked, laughing and proposing a headline. "Legislation Takes Bite out of Dangerous Dogs."

It was all in a day's work at a typical community weekly paper – except for a

▲ *The Castlegar strikers break out the bubbly to celebrate one year of publication of the* Castlegar Citizen. *Shop steward Karen Kerkhoff, Eileen Loukianow, Linda Anderson, Allie Chernoff, Chris Christiansen, Nicole Beetstra, and Karl Hardt.*

The front door of the ▲
Castlegar Sun *is littered
with Sterling Newspapers
TMC publications.
Castlegarians were clear
that they did not support
Sterling, They showed it
by dumping the Sterling
product on its front
doorstep.*

few little signs pointing to a big difference. The editor grabbed the phone and took down a birth announcement. Sitting on the front counter were two bound volumes, two years of the *Castlegar Citizen*, and they were autographed like a high-school yearbook. Chris Christiansen, an ad sales rep, had scrawled, "An amazing paper by an amazing group of people. Proud to have been part of it."

"Here from the start, here to the end," stated a note above Nicole Beetstra's signature. "Stand up for what you believe in."

"Proud to make a difference," added Karen Kerkhoff.

The high morale would be the envy of any manager, except for the biggest difference of all. The *Castlegar Citizen* has no managers. In the office there was not a boss to be seen. What did greet people coming in to drop off ad copy was a sign pinned to the wall by the door. It featured a yellow cardboard sun and scorecard: "The Castlegar Sun Strike is now in Week 127."

The people working behind the counter were on strike, but they were still working. They were also saying that it was the best job they had ever had.

The dispute that boiled down to a dime

THE STRIKE WAS ordinary enough when it started. One morning a knot of workers went out to walk around in the cold on what reporter Karl Hardt described as "a seemingly endless stretch of pavement on Columbia Avenue." The strike had the standard ingredients. A huge stubborn company trying to push a small group of workers around. Too much coffee, too many donuts. Honk if you support us.

But from the beginning it was clear to the group of eight (later reduced to six) strikers that people in the small Southeastern B.C. city did indeed back the people who put out their local weekly. The Kootenay region is union country, a place with a sturdy labour tradition. For decades miners and smelter workers, loggers and paper workers, have fought it out with hard-nosed bosses. The newspaper strike had its origins when the men behind Conrad Black's Hollinger chain decided to move into Castlegar in 1990. They brought with them deep corporate pockets and a notable distaste for unions.

Hollinger's new *Castlegar Sun* succeeded in driving a locally owned paper out of business, but in the process its managers pushed the staff – mostly women – into the arms of the CEP, which at the time was quickly establishing itself as Canada's media union. The way it happened is a textbook case of how bad bosses are an organizer's best friend. The people at the *Castlegar Sun* not only organized themselves, but also singlehandedly went on to drive Hollinger's scab paper out of town by starting their own strike paper.

The organizing drive started in 1992, when the small group that Hollinger had assembled in Castlegar got fed up. Management would harangue them because spending time talking to each other was, apparently, a waste of time. One publisher, nicknamed Cruella by the staff, would scold ad sales rep Nicole Beetstra for dressing "inappropriately."

Newspaper work demands strict attention to deadlines, and it can get especially tense when important news stories arrive unannounced just before the paper is about to be "put to bed." The same holds true for ads that come in close to deadline.

Linda Anderson, the production co-ordinator at the *Sun*, was used to bosses who were anxious to squeeze paid ads in at the last minute. After staying until 10 P.M. one evening, Linda was preparing to leave early the next day. This was before the union came in, so overtime simply meant time off, no extra pay. Grabbing Linda by the arm and wagging a finger in her face, a manager snapped that no one had authorized any overtime the previous day. Linda said, "Wave your finger at me like that again and I'll break it off." The scene threatened to get ugly. Her fellow workers restrained Linda, who admitted to having a short fuse.

The toxic atmosphere at the office did not improve after the time when Cruella took Nicole to task for bringing her daughter into the office. Nicole, who sold display ads on commission and also assembled the classifieds, sometimes had to stay after six to finish her work. As a single mother, this meant that she had to fetch young Felicia from child care and try to keep the tired, hungry little girl amused while she hurried to finish up. No one ever forgot what was said when Cruella came downstairs, fixed the cranky child with a glacial stare, and asked, "Why don't you just shoot that thing and put it out of its misery?"

This sort of abuse was not the only reason that the workers at the *Sun* joined CEP. They chafed at the rigid head-office guidelines governing what they could and could not do, the corporate formula dictating that the front page could only use certain fonts and had to have a certain ratio of copy to photos. If the boss wanted to run a wire story instead of a report on a local charity fundraiser, that's what went into the paper.

Then, of course, there was the money issue. The people employed by Hollinger at the *Castlegar Sun* did the same work as the unionized staff at the company papers in neighbouring Trail and Nelson. This part of the Kootenays is an integrated region where people work in one community, live in another, and have friends all over, and there was festering resentment in Castlegar about the big gap between what they were paid and what Hollinger paid just down the road. Nicole Beetstra knew what it meant to sign a union card at a

> If the boss wanted to run a wire story instead of a report on a local charity fundraiser, that's what went into the paper.

Felicia Harfman-Beetstra often came out to the Castlegar picket line to support her mother and the other strikers. ►

paper controlled by Conrad Black and David Radler. She lost 60 per cent of her clients – or $10,000 in income – the day after management learned she had joined CEP. The matter was soon resolved in her favour.

Despite the issue of pay differential, relations with management in Castlegar were so poor that the CEP unit at the *Sun* settled for strong anti-harassment language in their first contract, figuring that they would play catch-up next time around. But it didn't happen. In 1999 negotiations dragged on into the fall. Hollinger's offer was accepted in Trail and Nelson but not in Castlegar, where the employees wanted fifty cents an hour in catch-up money. Hollinger's generosity matched its sensitivity to the feelings of its employees. It offered forty cents and nothing more.

"The dispute boiled down to a dime," explained Rob Munro of CEP Local 2000, the media local that represents the workers in the Kootenays. Munro would go on to play the role of nominal publisher when the workers launched the *Citizen* with CEP backing. "It would have cost the company $1,500 over a year to pay the extra ten cents."

Disgusted, the workers started to walk the picket line just before Christmas. It was only a few weeks and a lot of donuts later that talk of a strike paper began. CEP dangled the carrot, offering some start-up money and cautious advice about how it had been tried before, usually without success. Far from being deterred, the CEP members in Castlegar dove right in.

"We just had the sense that it wasn't the company that puts the paper out, it's the people who work for the company," Linda Anderson said. "We were all confident we could pull it off."

In any case, she added, the previous managers "were as effective as a popcorn fart."

Facing down a media giant

THE SELF-MANAGERS took to the job of launching a new publication as if it were their own. Which it was, except that the little band regarded the paper named the *Castlegar Citizen* as an expression of the community that supported it. Linda took care of buying equipment and setting up templates. Eileen Loukianow worked on the business end of things. (Before CEP came in she had been hired by Hollinger at two dollars an hour less than the person she had replaced.) Employer solidarity meant that no newspaper printer in the region would agree to handle a union paper, so it had to be printed in Vancouver. Canada Post handled distribution that started at 3,500 copies and grew to 6,700. There didn't seem to be any challenge that fazed the group of seven women and one man. The first issue appeared on March 10, 2000, and in her

It was only a few weeks and a lot of donuts later that talk of a strike paper began. CEP dangled the carrot, offering some start-up money and cautious advice about how it had been tried before, usually without success.

Attempting to compete with the upstart *Citizen* had apparently been too much for Hollinger. The *Sun* had been reduced to a meagre eight-page sheet, half the size of the *Citizen*, which was brimming with ads.

first editorial Karen Kerkhoff described what was happening as "an incredible journey."

That it was: a handful of small-town newspaper people up against one of the world's largest media companies. When it took on CEP in Castlegar, Hollinger had 378 other papers and a debt of $2.6 billion. That was soon after Conrad Black began shovelling cash into the *National Post*, the most expensive political soapbox in Canadian history. In a column called "On The Podium," CEP Local 2000 president Mike Bocking pointed out that, rather than paying fair wages in places like Castlegar, Hollinger was siphoning money out of them as it struggled to pay down its debt. Vol. 1, no. 1 also carried a report on a recent Castlegar speech by Council of Canadians chair Maude Barlow, who warned of efforts at the World Trade Organization to open up public health and education services to private business.

The *Citizen* was careful, though, to avoid evolving into a vehicle for a single political message. The people at the strike publication made sure that it became a community paper, not a union paper. From the start its stories reflected local concerns. The staff made sure of this for two reasons. The workers wanted to give something back to the community that had supported them during four cold months on the picket line – the hot meals, the cash donations, the encouraging words, and everything else. They also knew that, to succeed, their new business had to be based on local people, local stories, local concerns. The report on Maude Barlow's speech was on an inside page, where it was dwarfed by coverage of Castlegar sports.

"The people who support our business read the paper and we're loyal to the community," said Shirley Gorkoff, co-owner of Pete's TV, which bought a full page of ads in the first edition of the *Citizen*. Two years later ads from local

The Castlegar strike ► *has its origins when the men behind Conrad Black's Hollinger chain decided to move into town in 1990. They brought with them deep corporate pockets and a notable distaste for unions.*

stores were by far eclipsing union messages, which at the very start had taken up much of the commercial space. Small-business operators know an effective communication vehicle when they see one.

"You've gotta give credit to the union, they've really supported those girls," said Pete Zaitsoff Jr, of Pete's TV. "They don't do any bashing. You have to walk the middle ground."

Still, the *Castlegar Citizen* changed the corporate recipe for appearance. Seven months after they started the paper, the workers decided that the usual photo and story would not do justice to the efforts of the women who had organized the Castlegar Quilting Guild's annual show. So they did some patchwork layout of their own and that Friday greeted their readers with a colour photo of a quilt that took up the entire front page. As soon as the paper appeared the office was flooded with positive feedback.

The staff accepted the compliments with thanks, but took even greater satisfaction from a story they had placed on page two: "Sun suspends publishing." Attempting to compete with the upstart *Citizen* had apparently been too much for Hollinger. The company said that its paper was on "temporary hold," although just the previous week the chain had gone to the expense of hiring a former employee to train its new editor in layout techniques. By that time the *Sun* had been reduced to a meagre eight-page sheet, half the size of the *Citizen*, which was brimming with ads.

Hollinger came up with an explanation that would have done Conrad Black proud. "Current B.C. labour legislation" had forced it to quit. The adjective "current" hinted that, should a boss-friendly government replace the ruling NDP, things would change.

Although there was much satisfaction and more than a few snickers at the office, the strikers saw things differently. Karen Kerkhoff's editorial took the high road. "We can't take credit for 'shutting them down,'" she wrote. "Hollinger did that all on their own." Noting the ten-cent difference that had separated the two sides, she explained the employer reaction to CEP's threat to go on strike: "Go ahead. Do us a favour."

Fellowship and the lightbulb moment

IN APRIL 2002, sitting downstairs for a quick production-day lunch, the six *Castlegar Sun* strikers (two had left for other jobs) laughed and indulged in some good-natured bickering. As they entered their third year they were giving off the warmth that a small group of people usually acquire when they work closely together on a common project. There was no longer any two-floor hierarchy. Everyone shared the same storefront space.

As they entered their third year they were giving off the warmth that a small group of people usually acquire when they work closely together on a common project.

"I have no problems with the noise," reporter Karl Hardt said.

"You ARE the noise," someone shouted. Laughter erupted as the women described how they were treating Karl, the youngest of the CEP members, as a "little brother." Karl blushed. Would it have worked as well with five men and one woman?

"It would have worked for ME!" More laughter, a few suggestive wisecracks.

"That's what I have to put up with," Karl said with a shrug. He figured it might have been blows instead of tears with a male workplace.

"Karl has had to adapt to a women-filled environment, and we're all pretty tough," Linda said.

Karen suggested that the whole thing had been a typical David and Goliath story in which the high level of community support was bolstered by a group of workers who told the boss to take the job and shove it.

"We've become what society has forgotten for a lot of years and that is the proverbial family," Eileen said. "We fight like siblings but when it comes down to the crunch we're all there without question."

Had any of them ever had an experience like this before? Nicole picked up the question right away, and the banter subsided as she began to talk. "This

Two pickets from the Calgary Herald support Nicole Beetstra on the Castlegar line. Earlier that month Nicole and shop steward Karen Kerkhoff had travelled to Calgary to walk the Herald line with their brothers and sisters.

THE CASTLEGAR CITIZEN

THE CASTLEGAR CITIZEN

◀ *"They slammed the door in our face over there and we picked up and moved on and made the best of a bad situation. We've made a good job of it.*
We've done it with the support of each other and with the support of our union."

• NICOLE BEETSTRA

experience, without these people, the last few years would have been even harder… I'll get all teary."

Her voice broke. A quick hug. Taking a deep, ragged breath, she continued her story.

"My sister was murdered. Then my dad passed away. I came back to the *Sun* and it was basically, 'Here you go, here's the stuff we didn't do for you.' I had a ton of calls and it was basically, 'Why aren't you caught up?' When my father died, I was at the *Citizen*. They took care of my clients, everything. That didn't happen before."

After a short silence Karen recalled apologizing for the strike happening in the middle of all of this. "Nicole said, 'You know what, Karen? A lot worse things can happen in life.' That was a light bulb moment for me."

Nicole pressed on. "They slammed the door in our face over there and we picked up and moved on and made the best of a bad situation. We've made a good job of it. We've done it with the support of each other and with the support of our union."

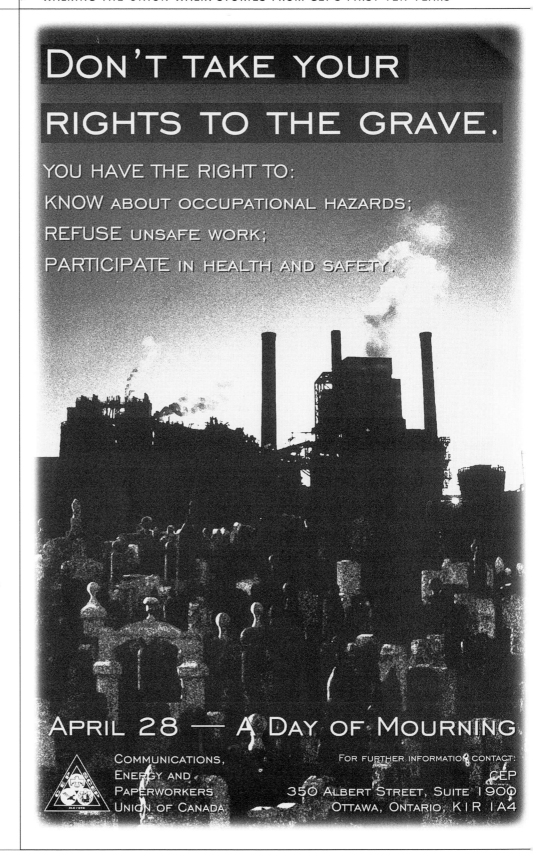

CHAPTER THIRTEEN

P. KEIGHLEY

Fibreglass dust and industrial disease:
WALKING WITH THE WOMEN IN SARNIA

THE MOST STARTLING IMPRESSION that I retain from my travels is not the big tires at the oil sands. Nor is it the deafening noise of a paper mill. What struck me most dramatically was a little storage room in the back of a children's clothing store. The space was crammed with racks of frilly dresses and first communion gowns. A tall box in the corner said "Easter Bunny." A toy pumpkin cabin was left over from Hallowe'en. The poster on the wall seemed utterly out of place. It depicted a grim graveyard scene with the caption "A Job to Die For?"

Sitting amidst the jumble in the back of the children's clothing shop, Sarah Ogg had been thinking about the years after she first arrived in Sarnia from England back in the early 1950s. She had a way of talking that sounded almost formal at first, but that impression quickly evaporated. The bright twinkle in the eye and the little smile were those of everyone's ideal grandmother, an old lady who had hobbled into the shop with her cane, looking for another gift to spoil her favourite nine-year-old.

She began her story formally. "My husband was the late Bill Ogg. He was a

▲ *Demonstrators support a sit-in by the Victims of Chemical Valley.*

159

"The sun was shining and it was just like a fairyland, all this glitter coming down into the yard. At that time they didn't have a top on the stack, which they got later on. I used to say to myself, 'Isn't that gorgeous? It looks so pretty!'"

very quiet man. He never brought his work problems home." It seems that even when he came home from London, Ont., after the surgeons had removed his lung and told him he would be on oxygen for the rest of his days, Bill Ogg never complained.

When Bill first started working at the insulation plant in Sarnia in 1952, "he had scratching," Sarah recalled. "He had put in an application somewhere else and they offered him a job. He said, 'No, I'm here now. I've got a pay coming in.'"

Like the late Bill Ogg, his widow has a matter-of-fact way of looking at life, and the facts of working-class life are straightforward enough. "We had to think of a roof over our heads when we came here. A lot of people at that time didn't have a pay."

Unlike postwar England, with rationing and shortages and cold-water flats, Southwestern Ontario seemed balmy. There were things called supermarkets, bulging with butter and bacon. Many of the fibreglass workers even had cars. What they didn't have at the insulation plant on Kenny Street just beside Imperial Oil's sprawling refinery were shop stewards, something no union back home would have dreamed of doing without.

Three years after Bill Ogg started at Fiberglas Canada Inc., the workers voted three hundred to six for recognition of union stewards and better pay. They started a strike newspaper. They put up a tent city called Unionville next to the plant, with a town hall where the workers' wives met to organize strike support. Two and a half months later the "Strike News" announced a "smashing victory." The company had to fork over more money and recognize the union's stewards.

Even before the strike the Oggs bought a car that Bill used to get to work. When Sarah needed to go shopping she would take the bus down to Fiberglas, pick up the car, and fetch the groceries at Loblaw's. Then she would drive back to the plant to wait for Bill's shift to end. She remembers it vividly. As she looked out the car window, surrounded by the refineries of Chemical Valley, the scene was pretty in its own peculiar way, particularly when the weather was fine.

"I used to sit there, waiting," she recalled. "The sun was shining and it was just like a fairyland, all this glitter coming down into the yard. At that time they didn't have a top on the stack, which they got later on. I used to say to myself, 'Isn't that gorgeous? It looks so pretty!' I absolutely believe that was the cause of my husband's death. It was the glass."

Sarah Ogg is among a group of remarkably persistent women seeking compensation for the deaths of their loved ones. Although the factory where these men worked was closed before CEP was founded, the union has been walking with the women in their search for justice.

Coming to terms with workplace hazards

BARBARA JEAN'S TOTS 'N TEENS is pretty well the only place in Sarnia where you can get quality children's wear without going to the big box stores or the mall. Sometimes when Jean Simpson travels to Toronto on buying trips, she also visits Ontario's Workplace Safety and Insurance Board (WSIB) to ask about the status of the compensation claims. In 2002 she and Barb Millett, her daughter and business partner, took an empty fibreglass insulation bag into the WSIB office. She pointed to the WHMIS (Workplace Hazardous Materials Information System) label warning anyone installing the product to wear a mask.

"It's like Kentucky Fried Chicken," she told the official. "They haven't changed the recipe."

Jean's husband and Barb's father was Bud Simpson, one of the twenty-five thousand production workers employed by Fiberglas in Sarnia between the time it opened in 1948 and its closure in 1991. Bud Simpson was sixty-four when he died in 1997. He had lost his job when the plant shut down a few months before he was diagnosed with cancer of the larynx. Jean nursed him at home through the years of radiation therapy, watching as the roof of his mouth caved in and the disease eroded his face. "If people saw him in the mall they'd avoid him because he looked so bad. His nose was big like a clown's from the

◀ *The Victims of Chemical Valley. Glenn Sonier with some of the Sarnia widows, a group of persistent women seeking compensation for the deaths of their loved ones. Left to right: Betty Dunham, Glenn Sonier, Emily Hicks, Jean Simpson, and Barb Millet.*

cancer that you could see on his face. He was so thin that he looked like an old man of about ninety."

Bud Simpson had worked at the Sarnia fibreglass plant, owned by the U.S. corporation Owens Corning, for over thirty-five years. According to the men who worked there, the plant was extremely dusty. Working conditions were poor, and production was everything. After CEP began to make its concerns known publicly, Owens Corning stoutly denied any connection between on-the-job exposure to glass fibres and cancer or any other disease. The company even threatened the union with legal action. Jean talks about a "gag order," about union people being afraid of losing their houses.

Reg McCurdy has not been involved in the long arguments about whether this or that substance used at his former workplace is or is not carcinogenic. He does know that when he arrived in Sarnia and started at Fiberglas after twenty years of working in Northern Ontario's mining industry, he found conditions that were dustier and noisier than what he had left behind. He also noticed that he would go home itchy. They called it "fibre scratch." Everybody got it and Reg counted himself as one of the lucky ones because the itchy rash would go away over the weekend. Others, who had the scratch all the time, were always oiling themselves and looking for some sort of medication that would relieve the itch.

The well-being of the workers, recalled McCurdy, took second place to output. Although he could not recall "the names of all the stuff," he said that he still had scars on his hands from formaldehyde. His story is familiar to workers down through history.

The CEP/OHCOW ► *compensation clinic attracted 168 people. Keith McMillan, the chair of the local CEP safety committee, helped to file ninety WSIB claims that day. Ten appeals were launched on behalf of workers whose initial claims had been denied.*

"If a pump fouled up or broke you went in and disconnected it and threw another pump in as fast as you could. You didn't waste time putting on rubber boots and a rubber suit and an air pack and all that sort of stuff. You did it. And you had it going in fifteen or twenty minutes. If you didn't have any problems and you got it done, fine. But if you got a burn on your hand or you got some acid in your eyes and you had to get an eyewash or maybe compensation, then you got trouble. The company would jump on you. They wouldn't jump on you while you were doing the job, but you got told after you came up. Production. Number one. Always. Speed the line up, make it go faster, whatever. It didn't matter."

After Owens Corning closed the plant and he was diagnosed with cancer, Bud Simpson began the grisly task of scanning the obituary page of Sarnia's *Observer* and making a list of the names of former Fiberglas workers who had been diagnosed with cancer. When he died in 1997 he was thirty-fourth on his own list. Before that he had taken his list to a clinic sponsored by the Occupational Health Clinic for Ontario Workers (OHCOW). Janice Holland, the clinic's Windsor-based nurse, took one look at Bud and his list and called in the clinic's executive director, Jim Brophy. The clinic people contacted CEP. One literature search, several meetings, and a few months later, some sixty former Fiberglas workers showed up to a meeting at the union hall, and it turned out there were outstanding compensation claims. A subsequent compensation clinic attracted 168 people. There was, it seemed, a problem with the old plant that had by this time been demolished. Keith McMillan, the chair of the local CEP safety committee, helped to file ninety WSIB claims that day. A further ten appeals were launched on behalf of Fiberglas workers whose initial claims had already been denied.

McMillan recalled that Owens Corning was not pleased that CEP was pushing the cases of the former members of one of its founding unions, particularly because the clinic attracted a lot of press attention. Once the headlines began hollering about health problems arising from the manufacture of a consumer product like fibreglass insulation, the company began to squirm.

"Their concern is that it'll impact on the sales of fibreglass," Keith said. "Their argument is always centred around the fact that fibreglass doesn't hurt you, it dissolves in your lung. But the argument they ignore is the fact that these fibres are coated with chemicals like phenols and formaldehyde. The chemicals the workers used in the plant were formaldehyde, ammonia, phenols, urea. Acids and caustics. They've always ignored the argument about

...continued on page 168

"They wouldn't jump on you while you were doing the job, but you got told after you came up. Production. Number one. Always. Speed the line up, make it go faster, whatever. It didn't matter."
• REG McCURDY

The cancer cluster

"TRISH SAID ONCE that if somebody tells you you're going to die, and you've got something to say, you'd better say it now. So we did."

What Trish Balon, Maureen Steeves, and Lorna Wilson had to say was that their workplace had made them sick. Bell Canada ran the place and said they were wrong. The women fought back.

They worked on the third floor of 66 Bay Street, a newish Bell building in downtown Hamilton, Ont. Lorna described the working conditions there as "really crammed." It was just like having a schoolteacher who wanted to get away from the old system of rows of desks; the company had arranged the desks in groups of four. Each of these pods was covered with phones, computers, fax machines, and printers. The work stations were so close together that the women didn't have to get out of their chairs to touch each other or tear a sheet of paper from the printer.

The women were plugged into computers that fed them a steady stream of calls, one every sixty-two seconds in Lorna's case. Although they worked shoulder to shoulder, it wasn't a terribly social workplace. When Trish was diagnosed with breast cancer at age thirty-one, Lorna only heard a (mistaken) rumour about how Trish's mother had died of the same disease. Still, she remembered thinking that it was a shame that someone so young should get so sick.

▲ *Trish Balon and Lorna Wilson, Hamilton cancer cluster activists. "The CEP called us 'sister,'" Lorna said. "Maureen and I felt great being with them."*

Lorna was forty-three when she got the call from her doctor while she was at work. She sat there with her headset dangling, stunned. It was malignant. Moments later Maureen was standing there.

"Trish and I have been there," she said reassuringly. "We'll all get together for coffee and a talk."

That's how it started. The medical appointments. The punishing rounds of chemotherapy. The meetings with Bell. Getting connected to the union. The friendship between three women who decided to speak out.

As a result of it all, Lorna became a breast cancer detective, gathering shelves of epidemiological studies and information on industrial disease and electromagnetic fields. Every file and binder has its place in her neat-as-a-pin basement office just off the laundry room. She is one of

Bell Canada is not a company known for its generosity or sensitivity, particularly when it comes to dealing with its female employees.

those people who are frighteningly well-organized. From the perspective of an information-based company like Bell Canada, she is a worker to die for. Except that the dying has been done by the workers.

Bell Canada is not a company known for its generosity or sensitivity, particularly when it comes to dealing with its female employees. In the ten years after CEP was formed, the company spent millions on lawyers to avoid paying women what it owed them in pay equity adjustments. The Hamilton cancer cluster is further evidence of just how mean-spirited Bell can be.

Early in 1996, around the time Lorna underwent a mastectomy and started chemotherapy, she and Trish and Maureen applied for workers' compensation. They argued that their breast cancer was caused by low levels of radiation in their workplace. They said that, contrary to the opinion of the expert that the employer brought in, having so many people get sick had to be more than a coincidence. The epidemiologist had acknowledged that the incidence of cancer on the third floor was, statistically, ten times higher than it should have been.

The women's research told them that pre-menopausal women in Canada had one chance in sixty of getting breast cancer. Yet here they were, three women on their floor with the disease. What's more, none of them came from families with histories of women having breast cancer. They had all had children when they were relatively young. They were particularly concerned about the specific effects of electromagnetic fields (EMFs) and the growing evidence from public health activists who argued that the increasing levels of chemicals and radiation in the environment might have something to do with the increasing incidence of breast cancer.

Lorna read everything about EMFs that she could get her hands on. She and Trish and Maureen demanded that Bell test the third floor so that they would know what they were dealing with. Ten weeks after the results were reported to Bell, the company let the workers in on them. The three women were not satisfied with the company's reassuring noises, so they kept up the pressure. Had there been other cancer clusters in other Bell workplaces? Could it really be just a coincidence? In all, six cases of breast cancer had been diagnosed among sixty workers, along with cancers of the brain and colon.

Lorna would later admit to being "extremely naive" about the caring nature of the company called "Ma Bell" back then. "The company was clearly angry with us for asking all these ▶

◀ *Maureen Steeves. When Lorna Wilson got the call from her doctor, Maureen said, reassuringly: "Trish and I have been there. We'll all get together for coffee and a talk."*

Joel Carr, CEP national rep and later Ontario administrative vice-president, worked on the Hamilton cancer cluster case.

questions. They started hiring all these experts to squash us full of fear."

The months rolled by. Ontario's Workplace Safety and Insurance Board turned down their compensation claim on the grounds that the scientific literature did not prove conclusively "at this time" that EMFs caused breast cancer. Lorna's files got thicker. Journalists converged on their houses, producing TV documentaries, magazine features, and newspaper articles. Trish had three young girls. Maureen had four kids under the age of eleven, and Lorna had one son. It was a stressful time, to say the least. Luckily one of the women had a different kind of job.

"Thank goodness Trish was a member of the CEP," said Lorna. "Because Maureen and I were in the CTEA, which is actually an association. It's not a union at all. It was the CEP that gave us our voice." Lorna recalled that the Canadian Telephone

"I never understood why it was up to three sick women to try to figure out what causes cancer," Lorna Wilson said. "I never understood why Bell Canada wasn't in there trying to help us every step of the way."

Employees Association threw up its hands, claiming that the Hamilton cancer cluster was more than it could handle. By this time they knew better than to place their fate in the hands of an employer who kept denying that it had any responsibility for their illnesses. CEP provided legal advice, documentation, staff support, and – perhaps most importantly – validation of their sense that, yes, they could well be suffering from industrial disease and that, no, they were not just hysterical women.

"The CEP called us 'sister,'" Lorna said. "Maureen and I felt great being with them. We felt like, 'This was a strong union willing to take us on. They're not asking for any money.'"

At first Gary Lloyd, Trish's local rep, took up the cause, followed by CEP health and safety staffer Joel Carr. The union commissioned a video to tell a story that was becoming increasingly well known in the labour movement. Everyone who met them was impressed by their courage and determination. Trish stood up at one meeting with the company and proclaimed with steely certainty, "I am not a coincidence!"

The months turned into years. Maureen would not live to see her claim validated. She died in October 1997. Trish and Lorna cried together and carried on. The way Lorna tells the story, Maureen had been the heart of the group, the empathetic one. She was the researcher and kept the paperwork. Trish, the most vocal of the trio, "the mouth," died in November 1999.

Lorna carried on as an activist, giving speeches at breast cancer prevention meetings, pressing the case for recognition of the connection between cancer and environmental degradation. As she sat in her office wearing a bracelet from a Texas breast cancer support group, she was gracious and patient as she told the story for the umpteenth time. It was only when she talked about her former employer that a sharp edge of bitterness crept into her voice.

"I never understood why it was up to three sick women to try to figure out what causes cancer," she said. "I never understood why Bell Canada wasn't in there trying to help us every step of the way."

If Bell wasn't, CEP was. By 2002 Lorna was still appealing the WSIB's decision not to recognize the trio's compensation claim. CEP was still paying her legal bills and bringing in experts to support the case that there is a link between EMFs exposure and cancer, even though Lorna and Maureen had never been members of the union. "We've carried this thing right through despite the odds," Cec Makowski said. "We're driven by the need to represent our members but inspired by the strength and will and character of those three women. I think it's our obligation to reach out beyond our dues-paying members to represent people who need help. If we don't do it, who will?"

While Lorna Wilson has no way of proving without a doubt that she and Trish and Maureen and Trish's union are right – and the billion-dollar company is wrong – she knows of one thing that happened that casts a shadow over Bell's claim that the illnesses were a coincidence, mere bad luck. It would have been out of character for a bottom-line-oriented outfit like Bell to waste resources. At first, when the company moved everyone out of the third floor of 66 Bay Street, Lorna was told they intended to rent the space out to a telemarketing company. The place was stripped to the bare concrete.

"Everything is black," said Lorna. "No lighting, no ceiling, no floors, no walls. And it's been empty ever since. It's never been reused." △

◄ *Lorna Wilson and Trish Balon receive the Clifton Grant Award for cancer prevention. Windsor, Ont., May 9, 1998.*

plant conditions and stuck to the argument about fibres being safe."

Health disputes between workers and employers often centre on whose facts should be believed. In this case, the company argued that fifty years of study had established no link between "workplace exposure to glass fibres and cancer or any other disease." Its ads in the local paper included numerous phrases in italicized, boldfaced type: *NOT TRUE, NO FACTUAL BASIS, NO CAUSAL RELATIONSHIP.* It even went so far as to assure its former employees that they had *A RIGHT TO BE PROUD* of their work.

The workers that CEP was representing – even though they had long stopped paying dues to one of its founding unions – did feel good about their jobs. Working-class people tend to take pride in their work. As former shop steward Reg McCurdy put it: "We had a good product. We made pipe insulation. We made decking for underneath air strips. Insulation for ceilings of flat-roofed buildings. Insulation for the firewalls and doors of cars. Building insulation from two and a half to six inches thick. You name it, we could make it." But the corporate paternalism was coming from a company that had left town and was in the process of declaring bankruptcy because of outstanding liabilities due to asbestos claims from workers south of the border.

The main fact in the dispute at Fiberglas Canada centred around whether the cancers that had turned up in former workers had been caused by the work they did. Jim Brophy and Janice Holland of OHCOW came up with a research

> The workers that CEP was representing …did feel good about their jobs. Working-class people tend to take pride in their work. As former shop steward Reg McCurdy put it: "We had a good product."

A CEP rally outside the Minister of Labour's office, in support of the Victims of Chemical Valley. Sometimes direct action is the best way to get the attention of the employer, or the bankers, or the premier.

P. KEIGHLEY

report from a study that focused specifically on 2,557 Sarnia fibreglass workers. The 1987 study, known to Sarah Ogg simply as "the McMaster," had been carried out by several researchers from the occupational health program at McMaster University. Although the study was unable to come to definite conclusions about the controversy over whether fibreglass in itself caused cancer, it did show that production workers at the Sarnia plant were twice as likely to die from lung cancer as were people in the general population.

Coupled with Bud Simpson's list and the number of men who showed up at the CEP hall for the compensation clinic, the McMaster study prompted the union to delve deeper into what had actually happened at the now-demolished factory. Glenn Sonier, a CEP national rep who had started at the Fiberglas plant in 1977 and moved on to become a union activist at the nearby Shell refinery, spent a year gathering information case histories from his former workmates and compiling the facts of life in the old plant. The idea was to document the case that, rather than individual bits of fibreglass dust being the culprit, the plant itself – fibres, formaldehyde, phenols, and all – was the menace. Then the union forwarded the information to the compensation board to back up the claims.

Glenn, who also remembers working in a plant where you always had to be cleaning up the dust, doesn't dispute the importance of keeping up on the latest scientific research about workplace cancer. But he also knows that when it comes to occupational disease there is another important source of information, one so obvious that it is often overlooked by the people who make decisions.

"The compensation board may not always understand the workplace," he said. "The workers are the ones who were there. Who knows better how the equipment worked, how exposures can happen?"

Industrial disease: a memorial and an occupation

THE MEMORIAL IN SARNIA'S Centennial Park stares downriver at the Sarnia waterfront. Chemical Valley is in the middle distance, the stacks and pipes looking like a huge meccano set. The memorial itself is symbolic. A family is set apart from the solitary figure of a man fashioned from iron. The nearby plaque set into white stone has a logo of a tear and the silhouette of a chemical plant: "To honour the memory of those who have lost their lives to occupational disease or loss of life due to work injury ..."

Jean Simpson, Barb Millett, Sarah Ogg, and a handful of other Sarnia women formed the Victims of Chemical Valley because they wanted the men whose lives had been sacrificed for production to have a place where they could

APRIL
DAY OF MOURNING
JOUR DE DEUIL
AVRIL

Sarnia is a town with a nasty legacy of industrial disease. The people not only live with the lingering fear of benzene and asbestos but also worry about the consequences of speaking out about those fears.

be remembered. Every city has its war memorial, but every year two million workers worldwide are killed by accidents and disease, three times the average annual number of deaths in wars. The idea came up after Jean attended a springtime Day of Mourning at the CEP hall. She had been disappointed by the attendance.

She said, "You know, girls, we should have a wreath or something ..."

That set the wheels in motion. The group found that they already had the fundraising skills they needed – they had been organizing rummage sales, church suppers, and charity yard sales for years. They persuaded local merchants to donate the hot dogs and everything else they needed. Other unions joined CEP in supporting the Victims of Chemical Valley, and it soon mushroomed into a community effort. They came up against a few problems persuading City Hall to make the park available for a permanent monument, but the women overcame them.

Jean found that they had something else to overcome. They had started the support group with the help of Glenn and Keith, but the men who had worked at Fiberglas Canada proved difficult to mobilize. Every place she spoke she found herself saying, "You men are the ones that could pull more weight." But she said she understood their situation. "The older men in our plant, they're afraid for their pensions. They can't touch their pensions, but in their minds they feel that they'll cut off their pensions. The young men are scared they'll lose the jobs they already have."

Sarnia is a town with a nasty legacy of industrial disease. The people not only live with the lingering fear of benzene and asbestos but also worry about the consequences of speaking out about those fears. Despite a legacy of job-related health problems, workers are accustomed to the neglect of paternalistic companies and delays from government. After the industrial disease specialists of the Occupational Health Clinic for Ontario Workers moved to Sarnia from Windsor, they succeeded in helping to win huge compensation awards for the men who had worked at the slaughterhouse that was the Holmes Foundry. In the 1950s asbestos levels at the foundry were 6,720 times the standard that would finally be set thirty years later. It can take decades for government to recognize that people are dying from their jobs. It can take years for compensation claims to crawl through the system. It can be frustrating for trade unionists trying to bring these issues to public attention. Riverside memorials are only part of the struggle.

Some time after the CEP/OHCOW compensation clinic had made it clear that the former Fiberglas workers were getting sick, CEP's Ontario vice-president Cec Makowski was sitting in the media studio at Queen's Park.

A single journalist had turned up for a press conference that CEP had called to publicize the delays in getting compensation for Fiberglas workers. It was particularly disappointing for Cec, because just the week before his press conference in the same place had attracted a roomful of reporters interested in what the union had to say about government parks policy. Clearly, industrial disease was not as newsworthy as wilderness preservation.

"I got mad," Cec said, and his irritation did not decrease after he left the legislature. "I was walking down University Avenue, spitting and kicking stones. It was disgusting that an issue of this importance wasn't attracting attention."

As he passed the office tower that houses the provincial labour ministry, Cec had an idea.

Several months later, just as the workday started, Jean Simpson and some of the other widows who had formed the Victims of Chemical Valley found themselves getting off the elevator at 400 University Avenue with a group of CEP activists. Jean had a card with the number of a lawyer in her hand. When the official in the office of Labour Minister Jim Flaherty saw the group coming, he locked the door. The CEP people promptly sat down in the corridor, in front of the elevators. For a brief moment the women were left standing there, until Jean said to them, "We'd better sit down too. It looks like we're going to be here for a while."

As the hours passed it became obvious that Flaherty, the man who later became known for proposing jail as the solution to homelessness, would be avoiding the office that day. The police did show up, but they seemed sympathetic. The VOCV women – who had left Sarnia at five in the morning – were relieved when the catering cart arrived. The coffee smelt good; the donuts and sandwiches looked tempting.

"Don't get anything," cautioned one of the CEP activists.

"Why? What are they gonna do? They've killed our husbands, now they're gonna poison us?"

"No, no. It's just that there are no bathrooms that we can use on this floor."

This provoked a round of laughter that helped to break the tension. The occupation lasted until the government agreed to meet with the protestors and hear their demands for a speedier resolution of the Workplace Safety and Insurance Board claims. When the widows and their union supporters emerged in mid-afternoon they were greeted not just by cameras and reporters' questions but also by a noisy crowd of demonstrators who joined them in a sidewalk solidarity rally. The CEP, it turned out, had ferried in a group of union supporters from a big Ontario Federation of Labour meeting being held in

When the official in the office of Labour Minister Jim Flaherty saw the group coming, he locked the door. The CEP people promptly sat down in the corridor, in front of the elevators.

When the widows and their union supporters emerged in mid-afternoon they were greeted not just by cameras and reporters' questions but also by a noisy crowd of demonstrators who joined them in a sidewalk solidarity rally.

Toronto at the time. From there it was off to the OFL gathering, where the Sarnia women received a standing ovation from a thousand people as they climbed up onto the stage. Someone asked Jean to say a few words.

"In public school you thought about it for days if you had to give a public speech," she recalled. "I was petrified. I just said that I knew that our husbands were there with us that day."

For Cec Makowski, the occupation was proof that militancy can get results. "We closed down their offices so that nobody could get in or out. They played it the way they do nowadays. Rather than beating us on the head and throwing us in jail, they began to negotiate. That's what we wanted." Sitting down in front of the elevators, he said, was more than just a militant action. It proved that, within a few short years of its founding, CEP had emerged as an organization with the strength and determination to do whatever is needed, that it can step in to help working people. There is no single way to do this, he said, "no cookie cutter approach to resolving problems."

Sometimes direct action is the best way to get the attention of the employer, or the bankers, or the premier. Taking strike action is the most obvious union attention-getter. But the head of CEP's Ontario region also pointed to another time that CEP members and supporters had occupied the labour minister's office – as well as Mike Harris's constituency office. In December 2000 they

P. KEIGHLEY

staged a sit-in to protest changes in the *Employment Standards Act* and the *Labour Relations Act*. The changes had raised the hours of work, given the government the power to declare that a union's collective bargaining rights would be "abandoned," and empowered the labour ministry to produce anti-union propaganda pushing decertification.

The year before that a group of paperworkers, members of CEP Local 290, spent twenty-six days occupying the bankrupt Gallaher paper mill in Thorold, Ont. Their effort to save the mill was in the end unsuccessful. But it was not, explained Cecil, futile. Indeed, that work is what CEP is all about. "When we walked away we knew that every rock had been turned over. And that's what we owed our membership. In the longer term, employers know that we're willing to do things that are quite non-traditional, that we're a force to be dealt with."

The struggle for a safe workplace

WHEN GLENN SONIER WORKED at Fiberglas Canada in the 1970s, the men sometimes complained about the level of dust in the air. It was just like at home, when the sun shines through a window and you can see particles of household dust floating in the air. Only there was lots more dust everywhere in the factory and no one knew what, exactly, the particles contained. The employer had a straightforward solution. They had the windows painted green. The sunshine could not come in. No one could see the dust. Problem solved.

"When you tell the public these stories, they're shocked," Glenn said. "But those are the things that happened in the workplace. To a worker, that's every day."

This everyday truth is connected to another fact of life that faced Sarah and Bill Ogg when they arrived in Sarnia some fifty years ago. They knew full well that a lot of other people did not have regular paycheques. Even though it turned out that there was asbestos in the plant, along with ammonia, phenol, formaldehyde, urea, and sulfuric acid – plus the fibreglass dust itself – Bill did not speak up about it. The need for the job trumps the need to protest conditions that make the job dangerous and often lethal. Workers and employers have little if anything in common in the tug-of-war between safety and production. As Reg McCurdy put it, "You didn't just take off because it was noisy or dusty. You had to earn a living and pay your way."

In the years since the Fiberglas plant opened, unions have made progress in the struggle for a cleaner workplace: WHMIS, joint health and safety committees, and the famous Three Rs – the right to know what they work with, the right to participate in decisions that have an impact on health on the job, and the right to refuse work they believe to be dangerous. Bob Sass is the man

"In this day and age, companies are bringing in chemicals all the time without proper testing. They're self-monitoring and the laws governing them are being reduced. The CEP has to be on top of it and be active. So do the members."

who preached the gospel of the Three Rs in Canada for so many years. As he points out, one team on the tug-of-war has more members. "Sass has rights, Rockefeller has rights. Workers have rights, management has rights. What does that mean?"

It means that the struggle for a safe workplace is always uphill, especially when governments slash budgets and employers applaud politicians who talk about cutting "red tape." From where he sits in Chemical Valley, Glenn Sonier sees the situation clearly. "In this day and age, companies are bringing in chemicals all the time without proper testing. They're self-monitoring and the laws governing them are being reduced. The CEP has to be on top of it and be active. So do the members."

Since it started CEP has been building links with the communities where its members live. That involves everything from sponsoring ringette teams to helping groups like the Victims of Chemical Valley. According to CEP president Brian Payne, "We didn't let the fact that we were a new union distract us from taking on the struggle. And that struggle goes beyond the workplace and the bargaining table and into the community."

Sarah Ogg doesn't get around Sarnia much anymore. She had an operation on one knee twelve years ago, and another operation more recently. It was a struggle to stop using a walker and get back to her trusty cane. Although she still drives her car, she counts on others to help out. She credits CEP rep Keith McMillan with helping out. He visited her in the hospital and now at home, making sure that the late Bill Ogg's long-standing compensation claim is still active. Because she and her fellow widows keep thinking that what happened to Bill and the others could still happen to young people, she tries to get to meetings of the Victims of Chemical Valley. She lives alone in a tiny apartment and has trouble making ends meet. Finally getting the claim recognized would help out.

"After all these years I've been patient," she said. "But I don't think I would have gone on if it hadn't been for Keith and the group. I'm a firm believer that there's something after this life. Bill said he'd be waiting for me." She knows what she would say to him if his claim is recognized before she joins him: "Well, I finally got it. You didn't see it, but I did."

> "We didn't let the fact that we were a new union distract us from taking on the struggle. And that struggle goes beyond the workplace and the bargaining table and into the community."
> •BRIAN PAYNE

CHAPTER FOURTEEN

"Globalization from below"–
A POLITICALLY ENGAGED UNION

IT PROBABLY WASN'T the best time to begin building a new union. But then again, all the CEP's founders had to do was look at what was looming on the horizon. All the signs pointed to tough times for workers, organized and unorganized, at home and abroad. Employers were on a roll as unemployment remained stubbornly high. Government's role – in ensuring a clean environment, a safe workplace, a more egalitarian society – was under attack. Public values seemed to be overwhelmed by private, you're-on-your-own ethics.

1992 The deepest depression in two generations had not abated. In its 1992 report *The New Face of Poverty* the Economic Council of Canada pointed out that one in three Canadians of working age "face the risk of being poor at some stage in their working lives." The adjective "working" was as important to the labour leaders as the frightening statistic. The high unemployment of the 1990–92 depression wasn't the only problem faced by working-class people. Even during the business boom of the 1980s, the number of households classified as working poor grew by 30 per cent. The food banks that had first appeared in the early 1980s had now become a permanent fixture on the social landscape.

▲ *CEP at the Summit of the Americas, Quebec City, 2002. The union is linking up with new international citizen networks that are producing withering critiques of how corporate globalization erodes human rights, labour rights, democracy, and the environment.*

It was Atlantic ▲
administrative
vice-president Ervan
Cronk who came up
with the idea of an
ambulance tour to
publicize the union's
support of medicare.

1992 The Cold War had just ended with the collapse of the Soviet bloc. The Cold War system was being rapidly replaced by a seemingly new phenomenon. Its advocates were starting to talk eagerly about "globalization" – not some new trend or fad, but a mixture of something old and something new. Free-market capitalism was still spreading to every corner of the world. But now the business bullhorns had a vision not just of a market economy but of a *global* market society. They saw health care and education not as part of the public good but as commodities to be bought and sold on the market.

1992 Global outsourcing, supplier chains, corporate mergers. Control over economic life was becoming centralized in fewer powerful corporate hands. Production, though, was being decentralized at home and abroad. Nike no longer even considered making its own shoes. Instead, the company was contracting production out to Taiwanese companies running Indonesian sweatshops. Information technologies and something called the Internet meant that distance and place were increasingly irrelevant to economic integration.

1992 Downsizing, outsourcing, flexibility. Employers were attacking job security, work rules, and worker representation on the job and at the bargaining table. Dominant corporations like Bell, Exxon, and Abitibi, which employed the new union's members, were pushing for greater "flexibility" by trying to have independent contractors do the work. At the political level, high deficits brought on by high interest-rate policies were being used as a lever to open the door to an even more direct attack on public services.

1992 People with the least power to resist – women, people of colour, Aboriginal peoples – were experiencing globalization's squeeze the most. Concentrated in the public sector and in unorganized shops in the North, or in export industries in the South, these people had always suffered from discrimination. Programs such as unemployment insurance and social assistance were starting to offer less protection to those who needed it most. People who did have jobs in 1992 told Statistics Canada that speed-up was colonizing their lives. One in three Canadians felt constantly under stress. Nearly half – and more women than men – agreed with the statement "I often feel under stress when I don't have enough time."

Time is money. By the time CEP was created, more and more unorganized workers were spending their time flitting between two and even three jobs. Meanwhile, employers were pressuring organized workers – particularly in the sectors in which the new union was based – to work more and more overtime. All of this was taking place against a background of unease about job security.

It was just the kind of anxiety that employers relish. The chief economist at the Canadian Manufacturers' Association put it bluntly in 1992: "Right now there is no job in Canada that is secure."

Politics and the ambulance tour

"TOWARDS THE END of the 1980s the future of globalization was more of a concern, and the union leaders, the founders of CEP, made the right choice," explained CEP executive vice-president Clément L'Heureux. "They decided that 'Whatever is good for corporations must also be good for the unions.'"

What was good for unions did not just mean matching the corporations by joining together to gain strength. It also meant being more politically engaged, like the Manufacturers' Association and the Business Council on National Issues, outfits that were making it their business to tell government to keep cutting unemployment insurance and keep giving more rights to multi-national companies.

Within three months of CEP's founding convention, Quebec members of the new union turned out in force on one of the coldest days that winter. The demonstration against proposed Conservative cuts to unemployment insurance took place in Montreal. In that city, one in four households was subsisting on less than $10,000 annually, and nearly half the people were living below the poverty line.

Two days later the new CEP leadership – Don Holder, Reg Basken, and Fred Pomeroy – appeared at a meeting of a House of Commons committee on international trade to oppose the proposed NAFTA agreement for total deregulation of the telecommunications industry and opening the Canadian telecom market to U.S. phone giants. The CEP leaders also showed how NAFTA would further cement the shameful Tory drug patent legislation that discriminated against domestic companies producing cheaper generic drugs in favour of foreign multinationals. They argued that this approach would boost drug costs and erode public health care budgets. The trade deal amounted to a corporate bill of rights.

"We have to learn to stop giving away more than we get," said Reg Basken. The veteran of countless negotiations was referring not to bargaining with Big Oil but to the supine posture of Canada's NAFTA negotiators.

The Liberals at the committee meeting lied that a government under their new leader Jean Chrétien would not ratify the NAFTA deal. CEP had just joined a coalition supporting a national child care program. The Liberals said they would bring such a program in if they were elected in the next federal vote. The program never did happen.

... continued on page 184

▲ *"Sometimes we forget that there are things that you can do as a union that are maybe more important than the things you do with your members." Tim McCarthy, a retired mill worker from Miramichi, N.B., drove the CEP ambulance in the Atlantic region.*

The CEP Humanity Fund:
Walking with Southern workers

MIRELLA RUBALCABA has been working in factories for twenty-five years now. She started at age fifteen in 1977, peering through a magnifying glass to insert sixteen hair-like strands of wire through a hole the size of a small crumb. Back then Mexico's *maquiladora* factories were called Export Processing Zones and were concentrated in border towns like Tijuana, where Mirella, her mother, and eight siblings migrated in search of work.

In the post-NAFTA era, the *maquila* sector – mostly foreign-owned – exploded in size. There are now well over four thousand of these factories, making everything from eyeglasses and computer components to underwear and auto parts. They stretch south into the heart of the country, but Mexico's poor farmers continue to migrate to Tijuana. Many of them have been forced from the countryside by the NAFTA policies that favour big agribusiness and cheap U.S. corn.

"Every day there are more people who migrate and have no sense of their rights," Mirella said. She now works coating lenses in an optical products plant and volunteers with a group working with women workers to defend themselves both on the job and in their homes and communities.

"My personal experiences are a big help in

being able to assist others in recognizing their rights," she explained. When she arrived in Tijuana with her family, Mirella discovered that her father, who had already moved there, had taken up with another woman and started a second family. That didn't stop him from forcing her into an abusive relationship with a stranger who happened to fancy her. "My parents said it was a cross I had to carry," she said.

Some twelve years, two children, and too many jealous rages and violent attacks later, Mirella left the relationship. Meanwhile, she had also left the job at the circuit-board factory and found one at a place that made computer and television cable. Mirella and her co-workers were relieved when the employer replaced the supervisor who never called them by their names, preferring a direct approach: "Idiot! Come over here!" But the new foreman immediately began to use his position to try to extract sexual favours from the women he supervised.

The company, California Precision Assembly, had a graduated pay scale that went from entry-level workers to the top level for people who could fill their quotas. The foreman got to decide who moved up the scale, and when. Although Mirella soon qualified for the top level, she didn't receive

> The group, Factor X, was just starting out, and as it changed and grew, Mirella Rubalcaba helped it along. The group's motto was "Women workers are human beings with rights."

Mirella Rubalcaba of Factor X in Tijuana, with author Jamie Swift. "I tried to show the foreman that I was strong and courageous and could face him even though I was crying inside."

the right pay because she refused to give in to the advances of the boss. When he realized that she was an upstart worker, he put her on the night shift doing several jobs at once. She spent all night loading, unloading, and stacking boxes of heavy cable.

"I tried to show him that I was strong and courageous and could face him even though I was crying inside," said Mirella, recalling the most difficult period in her years as a *maquila* worker. One day, she said, she felt so badly about the problems and her home life that she thought to herself, "I can't carry on any longer." She was driven to serious thoughts of suicide, even planning the most painless way to do the deed. But then the company eliminated the night shift and she lost her job.

That move resulted in an unfair dismissal dispute in which the women were betrayed by a crooked lawyer who took off with 30 per cent of their meagre one-week severance pay. In the course of this conflict Mirella met a workplace literacy activist who was working with a group beginning a series of training sessions for women in *maquiladoras*: labour rights, women's rights, how to defend yourself on the job. The group, Factor X, was just starting out, and as it changed and grew, Mirella helped it along. The group's motto was "Women workers are human beings with

rights." It helped her to become an organizer and a human rights activist who no longer accepted the crosses that her father and her employer told her she had to carry.

When Mirella first got in touch with Factor X in 1990, the group was organizing women in Tijuana's poor neighbourhoods, focusing on reproductive and sexual health issues and leadership training workshops. The women had little money. Their fundraising efforts included walking to work instead of taking the bus and then spending the money they saved on pencils and paper.

After 1993 and the arrival of NAFTA, Factor X – named for the female chromosome – decided to concentrate on supporting women who worked in *maquiladoras*. In 1995 it founded Casa de la Mujer, or Women's House, where it provided training, legal assistance, and medical services. Today it has a small paid staff and can afford to bring in a doctor and a psychologist. Casa de la Mujer can also pay someone to provide child care for women participating in its expanding training programs.

Now, after her shift at the lens factory, Mirella works as a volunteer organizer, leafleting plant gates, organizing educationals, and accompanying women who are standing up for their legal rights in the face of the pointy end of globalization's sharp stick. CEP's Humanity Fund supports them with the money it raises from Canadian trade unionists. CEP members whose locals have signed on to support the Fund donate a penny an hour, about $20 a year: less than a case of beer or a carton of cigarettes, the price of a good steak in a decent restaurant, or, to put it in more ▶

CEP members Bob Watt, Local 44, and Richard L'Heureux, Local 82, visit a refugee camp in Posoltega, Nicaragua. The CEP Humanity Fund worked with the Maria Elena Cuadra Women's Movement to build solid new homes for families who lost everything in mudslides during Hurricane Mitch, November 1998.

healthy-sounding terms, a fraction of the cost of a pair of Nike shoes made by pennies-an-hour people in Indonesian sweatshops and worn out within a few months by a regular runner.

All of this may sound like an appeal launched by a charity and based on guilt. But for CEP it is a matter of solidarity, not guilt. For CEP, the Humanity Fund is a way of dealing with globalization, of forging a link between workers both North and South. The fund is a new way of expressing the old union saying that workers are only as strong as the weakest link in the chain.

"I don't see it as charity," CEP president Brian Payne said. "It's a way for CEP as a union to participate with other workers in establishing unions and lifting themselves up."

Mirella Rubalcaba described most of the labour organizations in the *maquila* sector as company unions. The help that Factor X receives from Northern unions and non-governmental organizations like Horizons of Friendship in Cobourg, Ont., is crucial. Even a penny an hour

> **"I don't see it as charity," CEP president Brian Payne said. "It's a way for CEP as a union to participate with other workers in establishing unions and lifting themselves up."**

makes a difference. "We do a great deal of work with very small resources," she said. "With more support we can move forward a little more. We're in the process of struggling for a union that really represents *maquila* workers."

Factor X is organizing workers who are part of a global chain of production. The Mexico-U.S. border where they work is a microcosm of North-South relations in which multinational corporations write the rules enforced by governments and outfits like the World Trade Organization, International Monetary Fund, and World Bank. Poor countries sell labour rights to the highest bidder, and spend more of their incomes servicing their debts to the rich countries than they do providing social services to their citizens.

While Mirella was visiting Factor X supporters in Canada in 2002, Fidel Castro gave a speech at a United Nations meeting on financing for development, held in Monterrey, Mexico. The Cuban president informed the delegates that "the existing world economic order constitutes a system of plundering and exploitation like no other in history." He received a standing ovation.

Those among the delegates too sceptical to participate in the ovation might have looked to former World Bank chief economist Joseph Stiglitz, who said much the same thing but in more polite terms in 1999. Stiglitz, who went on to receive the Nobel Prize in 2001, was fired for his remarks. The fact remains that the twenty-five million richest Americans – 0.4 per cent of the world's people – have a combined income greater than two billion poor people who make up 43 per cent of the global population. This is the reality of corporate globalization. It is what the CEP Humanity Fund seeks to combat when it funds groups like Factor X.

"If large corporations are capable of reaching each other on a worldwide basis, we can do the same," observed the CEP'S Clément L'Heureux. "People, whether they are in Europe, Asia, South America, Central America, or North America, fundamentally have the same problems."

The efforts of the CEP Humanity Fund to combat global injustice by supporting grassroots organizing are matched on a dollar-per-dollar basis by Ottawa's Canadian International Development Agency (CIDA) – which brings up the whole notion of what "development" is all about. For the Humanity Fund, development is all about the French verb "*se développer*," to develop oneself. Development is not something that can be given like a charitable donation. It happens when people organize themselves ... sometimes with a little help from their friends.

Alain Leduc of CEP Local 501 at Camco in Montreal has travelled to Mexico. Like Mirella Rubalcaba, he has been a factory worker for twen-

MURRAY MOSHER

◄ *For CEP, the Humanity Fund is a way of dealing with globalization, of forging a link between workers both North and South. Administrative vice-president Joseph Gargiso.*

ty-five years. Although his local does not yet support the Humanity Fund, he believes it is important to continue making these North-South links in the face of the global assembly line.

"If we move American, Quebec, or Canadian factories to the South, it will never be to improve work conditions in those countries. The only thing that will develop is the companies' power base. I am very familiar with this reality in Mexico and in the South." Canadian and Mexican workers, Leduc said, "have much closer interests with each other than with the employers' goals." △

Anyone who visited a CEP office, from the national headquarters to the local outpost, has seen the photo. In May 1993 CEP made its first big splash on the national political scene. The baseball caps, hard hats, and white jackets adorned with the new union logo seemed to be everywhere. More than six thousand CEP members showed up in Ottawa. Parliament Hill had been converted into a makeshift cemetery with cardboard gravestones marked with the epitaphs of the workplaces and jobs lost to free trade. The membership boarded buses in the Saguenay and in Ontario's northern claybelt, swelling the ranks of the huge anti-NAFTA demonstration of one hundred thousand citizens opposed to corporate globalization. Don Holder stressed the need for trade unionists to build links with other social movements – with anti-poverty, women's, church, and environmental groups.

In the election of October 1993 the Liberals won a clear victory and proceeded to implement the platform of the Conservative government that had just suffered a humiliating defeat. The Bloc Québécois made its first appearance on the national scene, while CEP backed the NDP outside Quebec. It was time to take stock of where the new union was going politically. There was never any doubt that CEP would continue to stand foursquare behind social-democratic candidates. For Brian Payne, the collective bargaining gains achieved by workers over the years were, as always, related to decisions taken in the formal arena of electoral politics. Governments pass laws that damage workers, or they enact measures that help them organize and protect them on the job.

"Whether it be medicare, labour code changes provincially or federally, trade arrangements or corporate concentration in our industries, we have a much more demanding role than we ever did," he said. "Without those measures continuing, without decent workers' compensation, decent labour legislation, our collective bargaining relationship may be pretty hollow."

BOTTOM LEFT ▼

CEP's ambulance brings Alberta the message that U.S.-style market medicine is not only unfair, but also much more expensive than Canada's public system.

BOTTOM RIGHT

A light-hearted take on a serious business. The 1996 convention is treated to a comedy routine about medicare and the union's ambulance tour campaign.

At the same time, globalization and the rise of you're-on-your-own corporate values meant that a politically engaged union had to do more than call a demonstration, call a lawyer, or call on some volunteers to help out at election time every four years. This was the reasoning behind CEP's innovative Social Programs Campaign. If the union wanted to take its message to citizens in places where its members worked and lived, it would have to do something different. Most people, including trade unionists, do not board buses to go to demonstrations or help out in elections.

So in 1995 CEP organized a cross-country tour featuring five ambulances. The symbolism was clear. "Med-I-Care, the Liberals don't." The ambulance tour visited 125 communities, meeting people at malls, union halls, and churches. The ambulance attendants distributed material comparing Canadian health care to what was on offer in the United States. One of the vehicles was driven by Tim McCarthy, a retired millworker from Miramichi, N.B.

"I got a call from Elmo Whittom one night," Tim recalled. Elmo Whittom, the Atlantic regional vice-president, asked him, "How would you like to go on a trip?" Tim would soon find himself in an aging ambulance driving across Newfoundland on a dark November night. "Sometimes we forget," Tim said, "that there are things that you can do as a union that are maybe more important than the things you do with your members."

Tim, a soft-spoken man from Ireland, is a lifetime union activist. Soon after the first McDonald's came to the Miramichi, he took his four children in to see what all the fuss was about. When he saw a man in a suit holding a stopwatch,

The ambulance tour visited 125 communities, meeting people at malls, union halls, and churches. The ambulance attendants distributed material comparing Canadian health care to what was on offer in the United States.

he asked what the hell he was doing. Informed that they had to lay someone off, Tim turned on his heel and took the kids out before they could order a Big Mac.

"I explained to them that one of those girls was going to lose her job because she was slower than the others. I asked the little guys, 'What do you think of that?'"

"That's not right, daddy."

"We're not going back in there."

Tim never did return. Motivated by those same values, he drove the old ambulance across the Atlantic region. He started at Signal Hill, Nfld., and went along from there, telling people in every stop – from Grand Falls to Corner Brook, Halifax, New Glasgow, Fredericton, Moncton, Bathurst, Dalhousie, Chandler, and a dozen other places – about the dangers of a two-tier health system that would protect those who could afford care and tell the rest "You're On Your Own."

Local CEP reps did the advance organizing. Tim would have some people to speak to and some press coverage lined up when he got to town with his petitions, leaflets, and message that U.S.-style market medicine was not only unfair, but also much more expensive than Canada's public system. Tim had a lot of ground to cover and the schedule was tight. When he fell behind he didn't hesitate to flip the switch for the flashing lights and siren and watch the traffic pull over to let him by.

By the time of the ambulance tour it had become clear that the Chrétien Liberals were following the Mulroney wrecking crew. Finance Minister Paul Martin's 1995 budget put the axe to key social programs as he dumped the task of eliminating the deficit onto the backs of the unemployed. Indeed, the huge surplus in the UI fund created by his cuts to unemployment insurance was an indispensable element in the elimination of the deficit. The UI changes targeted "repeat" users, treating them like repeat offenders. As a result, given

BOTTOM, LEFT ▼
CEP's Med-I-Care campaign attracted wide attention. Feminist activist Sunera Thobani supports the ambulance tour in Toronto.
BOTTOM, MIDDLE
Brian Payne at Scott Paper in New Westminster when the ambulance tour hit town.
BOTTOM, RIGHT
In Fredericton, Elmo Whittom warns of the dangers of a two-tier health system.

P. KEIGHLEY

P. TRACY

◀ The activists turned every big chinwag arranged by the rich and powerful into a carnival of opposition, with the corporate grandees huddled behind police barricades.

its thousands of seasonal workers, including many forestry workers in the Atlantic region, CEP members joined the front lines of protests over UI cuts all over the Atlantic and Quebec. They were especially effective in a Northern New Brunswick riding where Doug Young, a hardline Liberal minister and militant privatizer, was defeated in 1997 by a union activist running for the NDP.

The new militancy: a multiheaded swarm

CLEARLY, BY THE END of the 1990s something new was happening. More and more the union was being challenged to consider new ways of expressing itself politically. The change did not mean that CEP's support for social democracy was over; that it would stop lobbying governments for better laws on workplace health and safety; or that it would no longer participate in the federations that made up the international trade union movement. But it did mean linking up with the new international citizen networks that were producing withering critiques of the ways in which corporate globalization was eroding human rights, labour rights, democracy, and the environment. Some called the new networks NGOs. Others referred to them as international civil society. Sometimes the new opposition was called "globalization from below." For people who weren't paying as much attention, phrases like "the Battle of Seattle" or "the fence at Quebec City" rang a bell.

But the opposition has taken many forms beyond the high-profile mass demonstrations at meetings of the G8 or World Bank or at the Summit of the Americas. The movement emerged as everyone from local church activists to big international human rights organizations linked up on-line and at any number of meetings to successfully push for a ban on land mines and to

... continued on page 195

The movement emerged as everyone from local church activists to big international human rights organizations linked up on-line and at any number of meetings to successfully push for a ban on land mines and to squash the Multilateral Agreement on Investment.

Investing in Le Fonds de solidarité FTQ

FOUNDED IN 1983 in the wake of the depression that left 14 per cent of Quebec's workforce unemployed, the Fonds de solidarité FTQ has grown into a $4.6 billion financial powerhouse. As a principal affiliate of the Fédération des travailleurs et travailleuses du Québec (FTQ, or the Quebec Federation of Labour), CEP is a long-time partner in the venture-capital corporation that one Quebec journalist dubbed a *"curieux cocktail capitalo-socialiste."*

The cocktail's capitalist ingredient is the fund's ability to make investments that provide its shareholders – the majority of them union members – with a fair and stable return on their long-term retirement investments. The recipe's socialist aspect is evident in the fund's name and its unique grassroots marketing strategy. It raises capital by appealing to the solidarity of Quebecers attracted to the idea that their savings should be invested not in the crazy casino of the global economy, but close to home. By the end of 2001 the fund and its partners, most of them small- and medium-sized enterprises, had created, maintained, or preserved 93,026 Quebec jobs.

In the winter of 2002, just as RRSP season was coming to an end, Montreal office worker Linda Young decided to take advantage of the generous tax credits available to investors in labour-sponsored funds. But that was not the only reason she invested in the fund. A member of OPEIU (Office and Professional Employees International Union) Local 463, Linda became the five hundred thousandth Quebecer to become a shareholder in a unique enterprise that has come to play a decisive role in the Quebec economy.

"I invested in the Fonds de solidarité FTQ for three specific reasons," Linda explained, summing up the fund's successful recipe. "To improve my quality of life after retirement, take advantage of the tax benefits offered at both levels of government, and promote the job-creation efforts of the fund throughout Quebec."

The FTQ Solidarity Fund was the first labour-sponsored investment fund (LSIF) in Canada. It remains far and away the country's biggest and most influential LSIF, in part because of its big head start, in part because of its relationship with Quebec nationalism. The fund had its origins in a socio-economic summit convened in April 1982 by René Lévesque. The premier called for social solidarity in the face of high unemployment and the epidemic of business failures concentrated in Quebec's small and medium-sized enterprises. FTQ president Louis Laberge immediately threw his weight behind a new kind of union policy to deal with all the layoffs.

"We must respond to the crisis confronting our members and Quebec society," declared the veteran labour leader, who had built a long and

By the end of 2001 the fund and its partners, most of them small- and medium-sized enterprises, had created, maintained, or preserved 93,026 Quebec jobs.

successful career on a savvy mixture of militancy and pragmatism. "We must find a way to create and maintain jobs. Otherwise, what's the point of having unions?"

At the time Quebec's other labour centrals rejected the idea of a union-based investment fund. But in 1983 the Parti Québécois government passed legislation creating the Solidarity Fund and introduced a 35 per cent tax credit for anyone who invested in it. Robert Bourassa, the former premier who was then making a comeback as Liberal leader and would soon become premier, also supported the idea. Within a few months of being elected in 1984 with substantial support from Quebec, the Conservative government of Brian Mulroney followed suit by extending a federal tax credit to a new category of union-controlled investment funds. At the time the FTQ, based in the only province that had provision for such a fund, was the only player on the field. It never looked back.

Since then some two dozen other union-affiliated funds have sprung up. Some are sponsored by organizations that represent financial administrators, professional football players, or members of Canada's diplomatic corps. But the real labour funds that eventually followed in the footsteps of the Solidarity Fund include the CEP-sponsored First Ontario Fund, the Manitoba Federation of Labour's Crocus Fund, the Workers Investment Fund sponsored by the New Brunswick Federation of Labour, and the Working Opportunity Fund, sponsored by several B.C. unions.

Not one of these, however, has come anywhere near to matching the financial power and political

▲ *Former CEP executive vice-presidents, Quebec, Edmond Gallant and René Roy both served on the board of the Solidarity Fund.*

influence that allowed the Solidarity Fund to engineer the complex 2001 deal to reopen the Gaspésia Paper mill. Saving the jobs of hundreds of CEP members was one of the fund's biggest investments ever. In 2001 the fund's in-house team of investment analysts was also busy with other projects, including a new fund aimed at providing money for mineral exploration in Northern Quebec and support of a biotechnology firm specializing in cellular therapy for neurological ailments such as Parkinson's disease. The fund's $10 million investment in Canada's only worsted wool manufacturer preserved 619 jobs and created 50 more. The fund spent the same amount to support the modernization of the Kruger Wayagamack paper mill in Trois-Rivières. That investment preserved 450 jobs, most of them held by CEP members.

While its headquarters are in Montreal, the fund maintains an extensive network of "local representatives" that reaches into every corner of Quebec. These grassroots volunteers were crucial in helping the fund raise $782 million in new subscriptions in 2001. Unionized workers accounted for 84 per cent of the enrolments. ▶

The fund makes it easy to invest by focusing on payroll deductions. Unions have negotiated over 2,500 contribution clauses with employers, allowing workers to save steadily all year round while getting immediate tax benefits. Unlike most commercial mutual funds, the Solidarity Fund charges no administration fee or commission. New shareholders simply make a one-time payment of $25 when opening their account.

While "education" sessions conducted by the big private-sector mutual funds tend to be marketing schemes oriented to selling shares, the Solidarity Fund maintains an impressive education program with a broad perspective. The fund provides economic training for workers so that they can increase their influence on Quebec's economic development. It provides support for the FTQ labour college and training sessions to familiarize shareholders with the ins and outs of starting a small family business. Its VirÂge consulting service, free to all shareholders and their spouses, offers advice on retirement planning.

The Solidarity Fund's remarkable success coincides almost exactly with the rise of globalization and the accompanying ideological message that There Is No Alternative to market capitalism as directed by an ever-smaller number of globe-girdling transnational corporations. Its success at home in Quebec is a sharp contrast to the corporate voices that are constantly calling for fewer foreign-content restrictions on RRSP portfolios. According to the fund, the value of its investments "affecting the Quebec economy" more than doubled from $1.3 billion in 1997 to $2.7 billion in 2001. The Solidarity Fund will not ship worker savings to Mexican assembly plants or sweatshops in Hong Kong; nor will it get involved in currency speculation or other games in the global casino economy.

The Solidarity Fund's links to CEP and its founding unions run deep. Edmond Gallant, the CPU's Quebec vice-president of the day, was on the first board of directors. In 2002 the secretary of the board was René Roy, who worked for Bell Canada, helped organize the CWC, and eventually became secretary-general of the FTQ. For CEP executive vice-president Clément L'Heureux, who sits on the board, the "*curieux cocktail capitalo-socialiste*" has been straightforward enough from the time it was founded.

"The labour world tends to be socialistic. We tend to observe the capitalistic system from the outside, but the fund, by its very nature, requires managing money and is somewhat of a capitalistic component in a socialistic environment."

In other words, confronting capital in the streets with the anti-globalization movement is not a strategy that rules out controlling as much capital as the labour movement can gather up. That's what the Solidarity Fund is: a big pool of capital controlled by unions and used for social purposes, promoting employment close to home. ▵

> **The Solidarity Fund's remarkable success coincides with the rise of globalization and the accompanying ideological message that There Is No Alternative to market capitalism …**

How CEP spoiled a Bay Street party

THINGS SEEMED TO BE moving smoothly in April 2002. According to the privatization gospel laid out by the apostles of corporate globalization and Ontario's Tory government, selling off the province's publicly owned power transmission system, Hydro One, would be good for everyone.

Ernie Eves, who had just returned to the government as premier after a short but lucrative stint at a big investment bank, was campaigning to get back into the legislature. Perhaps he wasn't thinking about the $5 billion worth of shares in Hydro One that were about to go on the market, though he did know a few of the stockbrokers who were about to be enriched to the tune of over a hundred million dollars in commissions. His former employers at Credit Suisse First Boston were part of the "global sales team."

But that wasn't a political problem. Apart from the stubborn provincial NDP and a coalition of pesky environmentalists and labour activists opposed to the quiet sell-off, few people seemed to be paying much attention to the grand plans to turn what used to be called Ontario Hydro over to the private sector. As Eves settled comfortably into the premier's chair, things were going according to plan. The Hydro One sell-off would be a done deal in a few weeks. The Initial Public Offering – the biggest in Canadian history – was about to be launched. The underwriters were rubbing their hands together in anticipation of some easy millions.

Around that same time, though, the CEP's Fred Wilson got together in Ottawa for a beer with Steve Shrybman. An environmental lawyer, Shrybman had been pestering every union, public interest organization, and environmental group he could think of, arguing that the government had neither the legal nor the political mandate for the privatization. "I thought I'd harass Fred," the veteran environmentalist said with a laugh. "He was one of the few people I hadn't harassed." Steve was convinced that at that late date no one but a judge could stop the Ontario government from selling off the crucial public asset.

The two had met in Vancouver. Steve had been impressed by CEP's work on forestry, energy, and pollution. "CEP has demonstrated real leadership over the years," Steve said. "They've been very thoughtful in reaching out to the environmental community."

Fred was intrigued by the thought of taking the Tories to court. The next day he passed the idea on to CEP secretary-treasurer André Foucault, who had been actively supporting NDP leader

Apart from the stubborn provincial NDP and a coalition of pesky environmentalists and labour activists opposed to the quiet sell-off, few people seemed to be paying much attention to the grand plans to turn what used to be called Ontario Hydro over to the private sector.

Howard Hampton's efforts to take the Tories to task for their fire sale of one of the world's most dependable electrical systems.

Hampton had been stumping the province for months in his Power Bus, pointing to his bar graph that showed how low Ontario power prices (8.56 cents per kilowatt hour in Toronto) were compared to those in the neighbouring U.S. states (35.28 cents in New York) where the privatizers wanted to sell electricity. "If you were a company operating a privatized generating station," Hampton would ask, pointing to the graph, "would you sell power at this price, or at this one? Would you sell it here? Or here?"

The privatizers based their position on two arguments, a combination of ideology and greed. They said that Ontario Hydro's big debt was due to its public ownership ("inefficient") when the debt was actually due to the careless overbuilding of nuclear power stations. The private utilities in the United States had followed that same approach, made the same error, and similarly gone into big debt. The privatizers also argued that the power system needed new money, which only private operators could attract. They made this argument even though public utilities like Hydro Québec never have any trouble floating bond issues.

For André Foucault, Cecil Makowski, and Brian Payne, the issue was another case of governments believing in the privatized, globalized future that ignores the needs of their own citizens. At a hastily called Sunday morning meeting in Payne's office, they decided that taking the Tories to court would give privatization opponents a boost

▲ *To the surprise of many – not least the Bay Street grandees poised to make a killing on the Hydro One IPO – the court ruled that Ontario had no authority to sell the company. Cec Makowski speaks to the media after the ruling.*

in the campaign to derail the Tory scheme. So CEP immediately got on board, adding the legal challenge to its support of the political campaign in favour of keeping electricity public. Although CEP initiated the court case, it undertook the effort in partnership with the Canadian Union of Public Employees. CUPE had already thrown its weight into the campaign against privatization by supporting the Ontario Electricity Coalition.

"The Hydro privatization is all about buying into the World Trade Organization and the globalization effort," André said. "Our governments have decided to abandon their responsibilities. They're saying they want out. We're saying, 'You can't do that.'"

On April 19 Mr. Justice Arthur Gans agreed. To the surprise of many – not least the Bay Street ▶

"Hydro privatization is all about buying into the World Trade Organization and the globalization effort," says André Foucault. *"Our governments have decided to abandon their responsibilities. They're saying they want out. We're saying, 'You can't do that.'"*

opportunists poised to make a killing on the Hydro One IPO – the court ruled that the unions were right. Ontario had no authority to sell the company. The judgment completely derailed the privatization scheme and knocked Eves's new government off balance.

Public concern about just what was going on behind those closed doors began to mount as the government scrambled to answer questions about the $350,000 yacht and multi-million-dollar salaries and severance packages enjoyed by Hydro One executives. Although the Tories soon had to replace the utility's board, their polling told them that the big questions remained.

The court ruled that the unions were right. Ontario had no authority to sell the company.

People were worried about the price of power in a competitive market. The cost was already on the way up. The activists supporting public power stepped up their arguments with renewed vigour. They pointed out the absurdity of claiming that homeowners could get cheaper power after profit was added to the cost structure. What's more, the government was planning big exports to the United States. It would be very hard to return to homemade power policies – and power prices – once NAFTA kicked in. If the system fell into

private hands, corporations would have every incentive to run dirty generating stations full out, selling electricity to power-starved U.S. customers and leaving the smog in Ontario.

Before the Hydro One judgment galvanized public opinion, the Ontario government simply ignored such concerns. Its leaders and minions were so confident that they were uncharacteristically candid about their energy policies. (These, after all, were the people who abolished rent control and called it the *Tenant Protection Act*.) Former Ontario energy minister Jim Wilson was certainly clear on the approach. "The private sector asked us to get out of large-scale government conservation programs," he said, adding that these programs "may have made the odd person feel good, but they had absolutely no effect."

Floyd Laughren sat as an NDP MPP for twenty-five years (five as Ontario treasurer) before being appointed chair of the Ontario Energy Board by the Tories. A few months before CEP's court challenge to the power privatization scheme, he said how surprised he was that the thing was not making political waves: "In all my years in public life I have never witnessed so little comment or resistance to such a massive public policy change."

All of that changed when Fred and Steve got together one day in Ottawa to have a beer. ◬

squash the Multilateral Agreement on Investment. The activists forced corporations like Nike and Monsanto onto the defensive. They put Third World debt bondage front and centre. They turned every big chinwag arranged by the rich and powerful into a carnival of opposition, with the corporate grandees huddled behind police barricades. Even though the slogan "think globally, act locally" got a bit frayed around the edges, the new activist energies were carefully directed not just at the prominent big international meetings but also at all the small local struggles that participants – including labour activists – saw as equally important elements in a new movement for change.

After globalization's opponents shut down the 1999 World Trade Organization meetings in Seattle, the influential British business magazine *The Economist* spoke of "an NGO swarm" to describe the groundswell. "Such groups are awful for governments to deal with," said the conservative weekly. "An NGO swarm has no central leadership or command structure; it is multi-headed, impossible to decapitate. And it can sting a victim to death."

The new political dynamism was similar to the energy that in 1993 had brought a hundred thousand people to Ottawa in opposition to NAFTA. But it was also different. The rally on Parliament Hill was very much a labour affair. The new militancy certainly included unions and labour activists, but the multiheaded swarm was broader, with broader political appeal. As such it provided both challenge and opportunity to unions, and CEP seized both. It was not always easy, for the culture of a trade union rooted among mostly male, mostly industrial workers is different from that of amorphous cross-class coalitions that include retired teachers from the Council of Canadians, young tattooed activists, and dozens of other formations – from the Radical Cheerleaders to Raging Grannies and the Revolutionary Knitting Circle.

> The new militancy certainly included unions and labour activists, but the multiheaded swarm was broader, with broader political appeal. As such it provided both challenge and opportunity to unions, and CEP seized both.

R. HATFIELD

◀ *CEP staff members demonstrate with the Revolutionary Knitting Circle against the G8, June 2002, Ottawa.*

The new activism of the ▲ 1990s was based on the need for social justice and a healthy environment. President Brian Payne addresses an anti-G8 rally in Calgary.

CEP did not hesitate to lend its organizing expertise and financial support to a wide range of political activities. The efforts came not simply in the formal political arena of parties and elections, nor were they just the day-to-day work of servicing the membership. "This is not just about business unionism as some people define it," said Brian Payne in describing CEP's political activity around privatization and deregulation. "I think social justice is a good way to describe it."

Describing it in that sort of a broad fashion made sense for a thousand CEP members who joined the protests at the Quebec City Summit of the Americas in 2001. One of those protestors was Western vice-president Dave Coles, who had been to the Battle of Seattle. He went to Quebec City because he was appalled by the secrecy surrounding the meetings where politicians and corporate executives assembled behind closed doors to make decisions that would have an impact on so many people's lives. When he arrived in the Quebec capital, Dave was "shocked and dismayed" by the huge fence and the massive police and paramilitary presence. He was among the many unarmed protestors who were blocks away from the security fence when they were attacked by the police and the military. A year after the event, Dave still could not hold back the tears as he recalled the brutality and the total disregard for the right to peaceful protest.

CEP's Western ▼ vice-president was at the Battle of Seattle and the Quebec City Summit of the Americas protests. The experience spurred him to urge CEP to organize demonstrations against the Kananaskis G8 summit. Dave Coles at a G8 snake march protest, Calgary, June 2002.

ELAINE BRIERE

"It was a very emotional time for me," said Dave. "We were blocks away from the action, long before there was any trouble. The government, the military, were firing rockets containing tear-gas bombs above the heads of school children and teachers sitting, protesting with flowers." He couldn't believe what happened next. Helicopters arrived to hover over the demonstrators, deliberately driving the tear gas down onto the innocent citizens. "It was the first time in my life that I'd have burned the flag," he said. The experience spurred Dave on to urge CEP to organize demonstrations against the Kan-anaskis G8 summit a year later.

The CEP's commitment to political action meant doing just that. It also meant connecting the dots between the union's support for the pay equity struggle by the women tossed out by Bell Canada to helping Mexican women organize unions and labour rights workshops through Factor X. It meant refusing to take sides with the petroleum giants on Kyoto. It meant aligning with environmentalists who point out that the corporate elite is keen on restructuring when it comes to putting the boots to workers but often silent about restructuring to promote more efficient use of energy.

The new activism of the 1990s was, in essence, based on the need for social justice and a healthy environment. In 2000 the CEP's landmark forestry policy made it clear which side of the fence the union was on. "Every environmental risk that pulp mills pose to their neighbours is also a health risk for CEP members inside the mill," said the union. "The owners of our industry have no interest in the long-term health or even existence of our communities and the jobs that sustain them. Our interests are different."

The same is true of CEP's defence of public broadcasting against attacks by the Asper empire and other privatizers who employ its members. That defence is not just a matter of doing the right thing by supporting the right of citizens to have access to information not controlled by private business; it is not just a way of defending the CEP members who work for public broadcasters. It is also a way of defending the public interest writ large.

"The privatizers want to do away with public broadcasting as much as they want to do away with public utilities, as much as they want to do away with medicare – anything public at all," said Peter Murdoch, CEP's media vice-president. Peter was among the media workers who protested at the Summit of the Americas in Quebec City.

"Along with that goes an attack on labour unions. The reason they want to attack labour unions is that there is no other group that has the same resources and the wherewithal to stand up for the public interest that unions have. So when the privatizers go after the voice of the collective, who do they go after? The labour movement."

"This is not just about business unionism ... I think social justice is a good way to describe it."
• BRIAN PAYNE

Photo credits

Thank you to the following people who helped to track down or provide photographs: Don Bouzek, Elaine Brière, Dave Byberg, Joel Carr, Diane Chester, Douglas Chisholm, David Climenhaga, Ray Cluney, Pierre-Suzor Coté, CP Photo, Yves Dumont, David Durning, *The Globe and Mail*, J. Gorman, Diane Gratton, Steve Griffith, Greg Moore, Steve Johnson, Robert Hatfield, G. Hill Photo Inc, Serge Jongué, Brad Jourdin, Paul Keighley, Karen Kerkhoff, *Castlegar Citizen*, Mike Lambert, Greg Locke, Raymond Louie, Don MacNeil, Murray Mosher, Imre Muranyi, Keith Newman, Brian Payne, Pierre Rose, Claude Roy, Bill Saunders, Ron Smith, Wendy Sol, Glenn Sonier, Jamie Swift, *The Spectator*, Pat Tracy, Carol Wall, Michelle Walsh, Joie Warnock, Julie White, Fred Wilson, Lorna Wilson.

Every effort has been made to acknowledge correctly and contact the source and/or copyright holder of each picture. We apologise for any unintentional errors or omissions, which will be corrected in future editions of this book.

Walking the union walk in Quebec City, April 2001. ▼

J. WHITE